WALKING THE TALK

WALKING THE TALK

WALKING the TALK
A Parent's Guide on Intimacy and Healthy Relationships

By Sarah West

Published by Wiseman Publishing

WALKING THE TALK

Dedication

To all the parents out there – cape or no cape

Table of Contents

*Each Chapter contains sections called *Questions to Ponder* and *Walk It Out* though it is not indicated in the Table of Contents.

WALKING THE TALK

Acknowledgements

To the woman that fought more battles than I may ever know and who was stronger than I ever realized until I had children of my own. Thank you for allowing me to "pick on" you throughout the book. There are so many great memories from my childhood that I did not share. I love how you held my hand every morning as you drove me to school and how you listened to music when you got ready for church. Any time I watch *The Godfather* I think of you and the weekend shared watching the entire DVD collection and eating pizza. Thank you for doing your best with what you had. I was not always grateful for your sacrifices and for that I am sorry. You are a good mother. I love you.

To my dear husband that has walked through hell and back with me. We beat so many odds and weathered many storms, yet here we are, twelve years later, a testimony to how God has worked in a marriage that statistics and nay-sayers said was doomed. You are my best friend and if it meant I had to go back through all the trials again, I would do it if it meant I did life with you. Thank you for loving me, for being a great father and example to our children. It is an honor to be your helpmate in life.

There are many people behind the scenes who made this book possible. Some do not even realize their hand in my journey. Many of the people placed in my life over the last eight years have planted seeds. If you have ever prayed for me, encouraged me, taught me, or loved me, you are part of this incredible journey I am on. Thank you for standing in the gap.

I also want to say thank you to the women in my life that took time out of their schedules and helped me breathe life into the first rough draft. Melissa and Karen, thank you for "red inking" my grammar. I was so nervous to let someone else read my work, but you both encouraged me to continue writing out my thoughts. Beverly, from the counseling room to the computer screen, you have been there every step. You always had the right words to say to me. I owe you the title of the book!

And to my wonderful book team. Abby Creel, you are a great friend and your help in the cover design means so much. Nicola Matthews, thank you for answering a zillion questions about formatting! Last but not least, a million thanks to my awesome book launch team. Thank you for being the hands and feet of this project!

May God use this book to promote not us, but Him and His truths.

Chapter One: Let's Start Walking

Your palms are sweating, your heart is racing, and your mind is playing out twenty different scenarios of how you will begin "the talk" with your child.

What if they ask me a question and I don't know the answer?
Worse yet, what if they ask me if I had sex?
What if I scar them emotionally because I say too much, too soon?
What if I don't say enough?
Is it hot in here?
Is the world spinning?
I can't breathe.

Let me assure you that your kids will ask you questions you cannot answer. Worse yet, they might stare at you like you are an alien from another galaxy speaking some cryptic language they have never heard before. You will walk away wondering if your children heard a single thing you said. As you lie in your bed at night, you will think of a million and one things you wish you would have said, but didn't.

Inhale, exhale. *Deep* breath.

There will be another day, another chance for conversation. The worst thing you could possibly do is to say or do nothing. You might be surprised that talking to your kids about intimacy and healthy relationships doesn't have to be awkward or even complicated. You simply must understand the role and take the necessary steps that lead to open communication on tough subjects. It won't always be what you say, but what you do, that matters.

Over the last several years, I have worked with pregnant teens in the counseling room and spoken to students on high school and college campuses about the importance of healthy choices. There is an obvious disconnect between their bodies and their hearts. And as much as we would hope young Christians are not part of the disconnect, they are. You can find reports that show the alarming rate of sexual activity outside of marriage that either back up our claims or debunk them.[1] The point is our message is falling on deaf ears and I have an idea about why.

When I ask young adults in church to give me the reasons why they were told to abstain from sex, I get three consistent answers:

1. Teen pregnancy
2. Risk of STIs (sexually transmitted infections)
3. God made sex for marriage

All these points are great reasons to wait, but these three reasons cannot stand alone. Teen pregnancy, STIs and sex outside of marriage focus on only one aspect of the equation: the physical component. But we, as human beings, are triune: we are physical, emotional, and spiritual beings. The importance of intimacy and healthy relationships cannot be addressed without fully explaining its impact on the other connected parts. When we try to make our case on the importance of intimacy and relationships based on physical ramifications alone, we lose them.

Teens will justify why they can have sex and figure out how they can avoid these physical consequences they have been warned about. Birth control of many forms can be purchased to eliminate some (but not all) pregnancy fears. Regular STI testing and monogamous relationships potentially lower rates of STI transmissions, especially if both young adults have not had other partners. And bluntly put, love, according to media and cultural standards, justifies the defilement of the marriage bed. These three reasons simply do not encompass the true purpose of abstinence, and it definitely does not even scratch the surface of what we should *really* be discussing with our children.

Do we need to be talking about their changing bodies, puberty, and the dangers of risky sexual behavior? Absolutely! But what we must remember is that real talk goes beyond lip service and starts demonstrating through example. I am sure if you are reading this you want your children to understand how to live a God-honoring life, in all areas. The best way to ensure that is to demonstrate it for them. If we want our children to choose life, they need to understand the importance of that life and from where it flows. If we want our children to make healthy choices with their bodies, we first must show them how to honor their bodies. When a person knows something has value, they treat it differently.

In this book, we will focus on the importance of setting the example as their parents. Our goal is to foster a healthy, thriving environment where our children can grow into healthy, God-fearing young adults. My prayer after you read this book is that you are strengthened in your own relationships and you gain confidence with your children. More importantly, I hope you are reminded of the important role and influence you have in the day to day life in your home.

This book was created for you to read alone or study in a group with other parents. If you are doing this as a small group, I would suggest that it be broken down into a six-week study. For week one of the study, I suggest you begin with a small quiz in the Appendix A of this guide called *Test Your Knowledge*. An *answer key* is provided. If you are reading this book with a group, make this part fun

WALKING THE TALK

– we are never too old for games and some healthy competition. Don't worry, it won't be graded; but it helps you gauge your knowledge and hopefully loosens everyone's nerves on the topic.

Here is a tentative weekly Bible study schedule you might want to go by for the remaining weeks:

Week Two: The Parent Hurdles
   Hurdle One: Moving Past Your Past - The Need for Transparency
   Hurdle Two: A Is for Awkward
   Hurdle Three: Is there an Expert in the House?
Week Three: What is the Parent's Role
   Role One: Encourage Healthy Self Esteem and Body Image
   Role Two: Model Healthy Relationships
Week Four: Age to Age
   Preschool
   Grade and Middle School
   High School
Week Five: Mixed Messages
   Purity: A Misunderstanding
   The Wayward Child
Week Six: Prayer

One point I want to stress is you do not have to be parents of teens to get something from this guide. This book was written for anyone with children or thinking about starting a family. It is never too early to start. I encourage you to take a moment to reflect and meditate on what you are reading. If you get stuck on how to talk about the material, or want to dig deeper in your own study, please refer to the study guide provided at the end of each chapter for questions and discussion material.

WALKING THE TALK

Go into the study slowly. Open up your home and allow the conversations among participants to happen naturally. We all need to remember that this is a topic that makes many people uneasy. Get to know the other parents. Relax. Then, each week, tackle one topic at a time. In week six, in addition to covering the Prayer topic, I encourage you to take time to write your own prayers, and to pray for your children. Prayer is powerful and even greater when one or more are gathered, praising and petitioning to our Creator.

The most important thing to remember is you are not alone on this journey called parenthood. No one is perfect. No one has all the answers, but we can trust God's Word and follow its instructions in our daily lives. God's holy Word will never fail us. Allow yourself to be vulnerable and let God's message infiltrate your heart, your marriages, and your relationship with your children.

Just do me one favor before we get started: Breathe. Inhale, exhale. You can do this!

"All scripture is given by inspiration of God, and is profitable for doctrine, for reproof, for correction, for instruction in righteousness." (2 Timothy 3:16).

Chapter Two: Jumping the Parent Hurdles

Before we dive into the true role of all parents, let's look at what is keeping most of us from confidently taking the reins. Our first major hurdle is usually ourselves. We have built a façade around us that everything is perfect and we have it all together. We are parents so we have to, right? Wrong!

On the inside, we are terrified. We have no clue where to start the conversation. We just are not sure if we can be *that* honest with our children.

Do my children really need to know everything about me? Can't we just keep with the small talk pleasantries?

If you ever want true, genuine conversation to take place with your children, they need to see a mom or dad that is not afraid to be real. The hurdles we face with "the talk" have never been because of our children. The hurdles we face in talking about intimacy and healthy relationships have always been because of us, the parents. If we can get over ourselves, we can jump the first hurdle successfully.

Hurdle One: Moving Past Your Past – the Need for Transparency

I cannot express strongly enough the importance of transparency with your children. Kids can smell a fake and know when you are trying to hide something. Trust me when I say, you don't want to stink.

In eighth grade, my high school participated in a "Just Say NO to Drugs" campaign. We went to the gymnasium for open assembly where we heard about the devastating effects drugs can have on individuals and the community. It got the wheels in my head spinning. Before dinner that night, I ask my mom if she had ever tried drugs. *Great* dinner conversation starter. You would have thought I slapped her in the face. She looked like the kid that just got caught with her hand in the cookie jar. Before I could even explain why I was asking her, she fired back at me, *"That is none of your business, young lady."*

My mother's intent was never to hinder communication with me. Her response was a typical one that happens when people are uncomfortable, but it was the end to what could have been the beginning of an honest and relationship-building moment with my mother. Her response made me feel as though I did something wrong, when in truth, I was unknowingly opening the door for her to talk to me. There are so many "talk" opportunities that could have stemmed from that one question, but my mother's retort and chastisement made it almost impossible to keep dialogue going. In my mind, I noted asking questions was something to avoid doing ever again.

As a mother now, I understand how difficult and awkward it can be to discuss all the not-so-healthy life choices I have made. I have two very curious children that have no problems playing twenty questions. But we are fostering an environment where it feels safe for them to talk and ask questions. Can it be awkward? Absolutely, but

WALKING THE TALK

through experience, personally and professionally, I see the power of transparency. What I am about to share is a true story, and the memory of this day is very fresh in my mind. I cannot help but smile as I type these words. It's also a chance for me to show you that my husband and I have learned to put our money where our mouths are when it comes to transparent dialogue.

My husband is a fire fighter for the military, but his career started in a city department. Before he began at the fire academy for the city, he was told to expect Human Resources to contact him for a phone interview. He expected it to be probing, but had not expected to be discussing certain things in the presence of our children. On this particular day, our family was headed for a day hike when my husband's cell phone rang. It was the Human Resource Manager following up with my husband's application. A phone interview of sorts commenced. The conversation went something like this:

"Mr. West, have you ever been involved in any drug use?" Without hesitation, my husband answered honestly. *"Yes sir, I smoked marijuana five to six times when I was in my teens."*

The chatter in the backseat went suddenly quiet. I turned around in the passenger seat to see the very surprised faces of our two children. (Seriously, I can't stop smiling at this memory. My sweet husband was a trooper!) My little boy, with wide innocent eyes, mouthed to his big sister, *"Daddy smoked drugs!"* My daughter immediately looked to me for confirmation. I smiled and quietly told them we would discuss in further detail when he got off the phone.

I am sure some of you are wondering if we really discussed our past "recreational" habits with our children. We did. An opportunity to talk about something very important was presented to us and we took it. It was a beautiful discussion that led to more questions and the chance to emphasize the love and grace God can bestow on everyone, even when we have done wrong. We went beyond just talking about the infraction, and instead focused on the infinite grace of our God to forgive us.

Sometimes, we don't want to talk about our past because we don't feel like we have been truly forgiven for it. God's word is very clear on that part. 1 John 1:9 tells us *"If we confess our sins, He is faithful and just to forgive our sins and purify us from all unrighteousness."* We don't need to carry guilt from the sins of our past with us into our present.

Parents, transparency is lacking in our homes and for many, it's because our own past is still haunting us. Some of you are afraid if you tell your child about all your sordid adventures, you are encouraging them to have their own. It's okay to let your kids know you have made decisions you wish could be changed. You are not perfect and never will be. Your personal past serves as an example that our choices have consequences and the impact can be lasting. I have shared the regret of sexual decisions I made when I was in college. I dealt with shame and regret for many years. When I was younger, I did not understand that when we share such intimate moments with a person, there is a bond formed that can be difficult to sever.

I am not saying you have to make an exhaustive list of your comings and goings, but explaining how you'd do things differently now could help them choose a different path.

Not admitting your own mistakes can easily isolate your children from feeling comfortable discussing what they are thinking, feeling and doing.

When your children know they can talk with you, it will free them to speak openly. Parents, don't slam the door to an opportunity because unresolved guilt from your past wishes to keep you silent. Remember:

"There is therefore now no condemnation to those who are in Christ Jesus." Romans 8:1

Romans 8:1 is such a freeing verse and one that we, as believers, can struggle with believing, especially when Satan takes every opportunity to throw our pasts back in our faces. So many times, parents do not talk openly about sex because of their own sexual pasts. It can easily feel like you are playing the role of hypocrite. *How can you possibly tell your teen not to do something* you *did?*

I have a past and many of you reading this book do as well. I wish more than anything I could go back to my insecure teenage self and tell that girl how beautiful, special, and deserving she is. I want to tell her that desire is not the same as love. But I know that is physically impossible. So I have a choice. I can share openly with my children about the wrong and unhealthy choices I made in my past, or I can stay silent. Personally, I believe silence is a killer of many relationships, especially with our children.

When I was still working with teens at a crisis pregnancy center, I received a phone call late one Wednesday afternoon. On the other end of the line was a young man. Through his sobbing, I learned his fifteen year old girlfriend was pregnant. After a few minutes on the phone with him, I scheduled for him and his girlfriend to come in to the clinic for a pregnancy test. To my absolute surprise, the girlfriend was a young lady in my church's youth group. It was a very emotional night for all of us.

The pregnancy test did come back positive and the young lady mentioned that she wanted an abortion. She was afraid of the shame she would bring to her family if she had her baby. Her boyfriend was extremely upset. As a counselor, I did what I could. We discussed all three of their options in detail and I closed in prayer. I encouraged them to sit down with both sets of parents soon. Later that night, the young lady sent me a text message. The young couple planned to tell their parents the next day. The entire night and the next day were bathed in prayer.

A day later, I received a phone call from the mother of the young lady. A billion different scenarios played out in my head about what she was going to say to me. To my relief, the couple was fully supported by both sets of parents, who agreed to help the couple raise the baby while they finished school. During the conversation, the girl's mother shared with me about her own pregnancy in college. The only difference was that she aborted. The decision had haunted her for years and she knew it was time to share her story with her daughter so she would not have to carry that same burden.

I praised God that this mother was transparent with her daughter that night when the couple shared they were expecting a baby. Because of that mother's honesty, the daughter chose to carry. Think how different that scenario could have been if her mother would have been silent about her own past. A life was spared and a bond deepened between mother and child. Amen!

We all have a past, but we must choose to believe the truth that we are no longer in the chains of our bondage. The grace that has been bestowed to us means that *all* of our mistakes, even the most painful ones, now serve a purpose instead of burying us in shame.

Questions to Ponder

In Hurdle One, we learned a parent's past can keep them in the bondage of silence. With your group or alone, remember that God does not shame His children. He loves us, even in our times of struggle and sin.

1. Are there things in your past that could potentially keep you from sharing openly with your children? Together or alone, read Romans 8:1 again.

2. What is condemnation? (If you aren't sure, read John 12:47)

3. What is conviction?

4. Why is it important, as parents talking to our children, to know the difference between condemnation and conviction?

5. Are we living like we know we have been set free?

6. After reading Romans 8:1, what do you need to let go that is holding you in bondage?

Walk It Out

Read back over Romans 8:1 and let God's word settle in your spirit. Give some time for the group to discuss their definitions of conviction and condemnation. In case you get stuck, remember that Jesus said He came not to condemn the world, but to save it (John 12:47). Condemnation comes from Satan and is meant to tear you down. It continually points out what a failure you are, and how badly you've messed up.

God's word tells us there is no condemnation in Christ Jesus (Romans 8:1). Satan on the other hand is *known* for condemning. Satan will point out your past. The first work of the Holy Spirit, on the other hand, is to convict man of sin (John 16:8). It sheds light on what is right and what is wrong. But unlike condemnation, conviction allows God to reach down and say, "Come to me... and I will forgive you!" Condemnation shows you the problem, but avoids a solution. Conviction points to the solution through the blood of Christ.

Why is this important? Some of your children may have already made sexual decisions. Many regret that decision once made and feel hopeless. They need to understand that regardless of where they are in their purity walk, God will forgive their transgressions. Many times young adults will not talk to their parents because they are ashamed of their activities and are afraid to face the disappointment of their parents. Instead of starting over where they are, they continue down a sinful path because they fear it is too late for them. It is never too late to receive God's forgiveness. As parents, we need to make sure they understand that we love them and so does God. When our children know they are forgiven and loved, they will make a U-turn.

It is essential, parents, that we not only speak this truth but *live* it. If we tell our children God can forgive and renew our spirits, they must see us living a renewed life.

WALKING THE TALK

Hurdle Two: A is for Awkward

Do you remember "the talk" with your parents? I remember my own very well.

I was in seventh grade. One Saturday my mother and I went shopping in a neighboring city. That city just so happened to be home to a large university, which would later become my alma mater. I really don't think my mom had planned "the talk" with me that day, but due to some other family issues, it just happened. As we drove in silence, we passed the sorority dorms of the college. In a quick motion, my mom pointed to the dormitory to draw my attention to it.

"Do you see that place Sarah?" I nodded.

"That place is full of disease. All people do there is party and have sex."

How does a gal respond? The images and thoughts that ran through my head as she spoke were terrifying. I didn't want to be one of those college kids that partied, had sex and got diseases. I was petrified. I was twelve-ish and had never kissed a boy at that point. The idea of sex freaked me out, and here she was telling me if I had sex I would become a diseased, party-crazed kid just like the hell raisers on that campus. I made a vow that day to become a nun. (Thankfully short-lived or I wouldn't be writing this book.)

There are a few things I took from my own experience with my mother. Though I appreciated my mother's valiant attempt to have the birds and bees talk with me, I knew that I did not want to handle it the same way when I had children. Try not to judge her. She gets an A....for Awkward.

What I did not tell you prior to my own personal "talk" story was that at the time, my sister, age 17, was pregnant. I can only assume this particular situation was a huge motivator for my mother's impromptu sex discussion in the car. Unrehearsed life discussions are not necessarily a bad thing, but the motivator behind the timing can be. So many times the conversations we have with our children are motivated out of fear, shame, and desperation. As parents, we fear if we don't say something, our kids will act on everything. Not true, but we aren't helping them navigate when we try to force conversation.

Our personal shame can make us desperate for a redo. *Sometimes, we see our kids as the chance to make our life right.* We over-compensate in their life with the hope that somehow the past will not repeat itself. Again, not true – we can't control their choices, or redeem our own mistakes through them. They don't need more options; they need God-fearing parents who are willing to walk through the good, the bad, and the ugly with them as they navigate life, all while pointing them to Christ. Remember, our motivators for leading our children can make the situation awkward in itself. There is nothing wrong with wanting your child to have a different life, but forcing the conversation can make it awkward and we don't want that. We want conversations that are natural and we get that by living out our values. I will never stress this enough, parents. Our children learn by watching us.

Do you recall some of the thoughts I had after my mother's impromptu sex talk with me? I did not want to be one of those *"diseased, party-crazed kids like the hell raisers on that campus."* What my mother said and what I heard were very different. Specificity is vital when having a conversation with our kids. I read things into that conversation that simply were not implied. I took away that sex was dirty and having sex would make you dirty. At age twelve, I envisioned a "diseased infested" college student resembling the zombies from the "living dead" movies. Yeah, not the most accurate description, is it?

Our children's maturity plays a huge role in how much we convey and when. We can't leave things hanging and assume our kids know what we are talking about. It might be clear to us, but not them. What could be a great conversation starter will be stopped short because of the awkward approach to the subject. Trust me when I say this. If we are showing them *daily* how to live out godly relationships and how to make Christ-focused decisions, we will find we have no need for all the awkward approaches and preparations. The conversations will simply flow and because it is so natural, questions will be much easier to ask.

Sex is not a one-time discussion that we can throw around at the dinner table and hope we never need to discuss again. Many parents make a valiant attempt to discuss the importance of intimacy and healthy relationships, but many times it's only one time. It is one thing to discuss sex and healthy relationships with a child when they aren't dating, but when the hormones kick in and the boys/girls start coming around, the conversation needs to keep going. After that particular conversation with my mother, there were no more discussions on safe sex, dating or boundaries. One time is not enough, unless we want it to be one of the most awkward moments of our children's existence.

Sex is a topic that is built upon from the time they are little and goes well beyond just something physical (remember, we are triune beings). Then as the topics get deeper and more specific, neither you nor your children will feel as awkward because you have been discussing topics on body image, boundaries, respect and self-control from an early age. The great thing is that you can tailor the discussion to their age level and their specific need. If you didn't start early, don't stress. Start where you are. The point is to start.

Not knowing when to start is where parents become awkward with their children. Many of us don't know where to begin so we wait until the most inopportune times to try and discuss important issues. I understand that it seems easier to wait until there is a problem (or potential one) before tackling "the talk." After all, why discuss sex if you don't need to? Sorry, but that approach has failed time and time again. I have seen too many parents sitting across from me in the counseling room regretting that very decision to wait to start talking to their children about sex.

We wait until our children hit puberty to talk about puberty. We wait until our children are hormonally charged teenagers with a girlfriend or boyfriend before we even attempt a discussion on sex. As parents, we are ill-prepared, and we wonder why it is so awkward to have open, transparent dialogue with our children. Ben Franklin once said, *"By failing to prepare, you prepare to fail."* I don't want to see any parent, myself included, fail at such an important task.

We have to start looking at the discussion surrounding intimacy and relationships as a continual discussion and our actions must speak louder than our words. If you don't know what to do or what to say, remember we have the greatest Counselor we could ever want in our corner. James 1:5-6 states, *"If any of you lack wisdom, you should ask God, who gives generously to all without finding fault, and it will be given to you. But when you ask, you must believe and not doubt, because the one who doubts is like a wave of the sea, blown and tossed by the wind."*

Parents, the words will come. You just have to lead the way. You can do this!

WALKING THE TALK

Questions to Ponder

Hurdle Two addresses the awkwardness that can be associated with talking to our children. Let's take a moment and discuss why we have made this important topic so awkward. Are there things we need to change? What can you learn from others on this area?

1. What do you remember about "the talk" with your parents?

2. What do you want to do differently with your children? What would you do the same?

3. How do you view sex? (Do you consider sex to be "dirty," etc.?)

4. Hurdle Two talks about motivators. What is your motivation in talking to your children (fear, concern, prevention etc.)?

5. Are you unsure how to start the conversation? How can God help you in this journey called parenting? Take a moment and read James 1:5-6.

Walk It Out

This discussion time is a great chance to hear other people's "talk" story. The subject we are dealing with can be so serious, and I find that sharing heart to heart at this time makes our load much easier to carry. You will learn what "the talk" entailed for each member of your group. Maybe you can go away with a few pointers.

Share what you would each do differently or how you hope to speak candidly to your own children one day. Not everyone will have a horror story, so glean off one another. Find what works for each of your families, then go home and own it.

Many times, people have a very distorted view of sex. When all you hear about sex from the schools and the pulpit involves a big fat NO it is easy to associate sex with something wrong or vile. Often times, we do not even realize that we have such mixed feelings about this beautiful act. But let me remind you of one thing: if sex was not that big of a deal or meant very little to God, scripture would not have addressed it as it does. It was one of the first commands God gave Adam in Genesis 1:8. "Be fruitful and multiply." Sex, in God's time, is a beautiful thing (Song of Solomon 8:4).

Our view on sex can be a huge motivator for us to talk about it or to avoid it. Wanting your children to make healthy choices in order to avoid an unplanned pregnancy or disease is not wrong. But as believers, prevention cannot be your only motivator. We need to teach our children about obedience. The best way that can be taught is by showing obedience lived out in your daily life. We honor our bodies because we love and honor God.

Still unsure of how to lead this conversation? Seek God and allow Him to direct you through His Word.

WALKING THE TALK

Hurdle Three: Is There an Expert in the House?

My husband and I homeschool our children. It has been one of the best, but hardest, decisions our family has ever had to make. I was a career mom, working very long hours, and "quality family time" was a rush through bath time, dinner, and a quick bedtime tuck-in before I collapsed from exhaustion. I wrestled with the desire to come home and teach our children for several years. Finally, after much prayer, I felt we had our answer after an incident at my daughter's school. Apparently, there was much more than playing happening during recess. Near the swings, the younger students were getting a first rate sex education from some 4th grade students. I will go into further detail later on how we handled that talk, but it was an eye opener for us.

I don't tell you this to start a debate on what is the better educational choice. I feel strongly that a parent needs to do what is best for their family. I am sharing this story so you understand that *someone* is going to talk to your children about sex. Who that someone is will be entirely up to you.

"The talk" can be hard to address. All families, across the board, struggle in their role as the "expert." My family periodically meets for a play date with some other homeschool families. Though we all use different curriculums to teach, we discovered that all the science lessons were related to the topic of reproduction. The conversation turned to the topic of sex and how and if we had started that discussion with our children (the ears that must have been burning in Chick-fil-A that day). I learned most of the moms felt overwhelmed even discussing educational based curriculum that dealt with the reproductive system. The moms feared they were not qualified to teach on the subject. One of the sweet mothers even exclaimed, *"I don't have a* clue *where to start. I just keep putting it off."*

I want you to see something and soak it in. These are parents that have stepped away from the conventional educational institution and have taken the reigns of their children's education. And though many of us homeschool moms feel qualified to teach trigonometry, we question if we are qualified to teach our children about sex. I don't say that insolently, but it was the first time I realized that the fear of being unqualified to talk about such an important topic was across the board. I often forget that sex is an uncomfortable subject for many since talking about sex is like second nature for me.

Here's the problem with thinking we are not qualified. When we question our competency to tackle such an important subject, we have a tendency to rely on other adeptly educated persons to instruct our children about what was designed to be our job to teach them. The Bible says to *"Train up a child in the way he should go, and when he is older he will not depart from it." Proverbs 22:6.* With our feelings of incompetency, we hand over the rights to the school system and many times to the church. It might sound harsh, but it is true. There is reason abstinence-based events are so popular among the churches. Parents hope that the events will tackle the subject of sex for them, and in turn, keep their teens from acting out on any physical urges.

Abstinence based programs, both secular and spiritual, can be a *catalyst* to help open the discussion. They are also positive peer groups that help children stand strong. I am in in full support of such programs as long as they are *supplemental* to what is being taught in the home. With conviction, I say wholeheartedly that parents need to be the primary educator on spiritual matters. *And yes,*

WALKING THE TALK

intimacy is as much spiritual as it is physical. Parents need to be the first person their children seek when they have a question. Parents cannot put the responsibility on programs that spend less than two hours with their children and expect lasting results. Allow me to share another story that deals directly with this topic.

During my tenure as a sexual health educator, I personally orchestrated purity events for local schools and churches. The turnout was always awesome and many teens made the decision to remain abstinent, or to at least stay abstinent from that day forward. Purity rings were sold to serve as a reminder of their decision. At one particular event, a teenage girl made the decision to remain abstinent and her mother purchased her a purity ring. A few months later, the mother caught the girl having sex with her boyfriend. She contacted the company that sold the ring to her daughter, demanding a full refund. According to the mother, the "ring didn't work." Yes, this is an extreme example, but it happened, and I'm sure she's not the only one.

As beautiful as I find the symbolism of a purity ring, I always stressed to the parents and teens alike the ring can only be a representation of their commitment. It holds no real power to keep them from going back on their decision any more than wedding rings hold a married couple to their vows. A one-time event or an hour in a hot school gymnasium cannot be the anchor that we rely on to teach our children the importance of intimacy and healthy relationships. The decision to remain pure is a daily decision, sometimes even an hourly one. The conversation has to continue, and it should start and end at home.

Parents, please stop putting pressure on yourself that you have to know everything. You know your kids better than anyone else. Start there. Before becoming a mom and dad, did you know how to change a diaper, fix a bottle, or properly burp a baby? My guess is no. You might have had an idea of what to do, but many new parents will tell you they were scared to death when they brought their first child home from the hospital. It's okay to say you don't know the answer, and it's okay to be scared. Transparency and open dialogue is what is important. Telling your kids you don't have the answer won't retract from your authority. In fact, your kids will more than likely respect you for being honest. If a question is asked and you don't know the answer, go research it and then discuss what you find with your kids.

I will admit that I learned a plethora of things I did not know when I first started teaching sexual health in the classroom. I got a first rate education on sexually transmitted infections. The material was there for my consumption, but I had to put forth an effort to learn it. It takes dedication, and believe it or not, some studying (depending on how deep you go into the conversation). The first day in a class full of seniors, I got asked a question I had no idea how to answer. Thank goodness it was a two-day session. I went home, researched it, and came back the next day and answered it. The student was impressed that I had remembered, and it also showed I cared. My actions opened the door for authentic transparent discussion to take place.

In all honesty, most teens aren't looking for us to be experts on the topic of sex. The mechanics of sexual intimacy come naturally so we don't have to be graphic on the how. The physical act of sex has not been tainted by our sin nature; our attitudes towards intimacy and relationships have been distorted because of man's fall to sin. The goal is for us to understand the importance of our role *played out* in front of our children.

From my experience, most teen's interests seem to revolve more around the topic of relationship building for this reason. Humans were created to be relational beings and our identity was meant to be in Christ, not of the world.

WALKING THE TALK

Our sin separated us from our true identity, and since then people have been looking for fillers through improper relationships. You can look around and see that our youth have a very distorted view of what constitutes a relationship. Girls don't understand the difference between being valued and desired. Boys are being shown that the conquests, and not respect, of the opposite sex constitute the definition of a man. What do you want your kids to be learning in the area of intimacy and relationships? Who do you want influencing them?

If the idea that you aren't an expert in the area of sex and relationships still concerns you, let me address it another way. Most teens use social media as their platform to broadcast their lives. In this generation, the advice and opinions of friends and those they hold dear in their life is much more valuable and accepted than the teaching of a man or woman with a Ph.D. When I first got into the counseling room, I questioned if I should be there. When I stepped into the classroom, I wondered how I had any authority to stand up there and tell these teens anything. Then I remembered: I cared about them and they knew that. I was willing to openly discuss the topic with them, and to learn along with them if need be.

You can get numerous books (including this one) that can help you prepare for "the talk", but it's your hearts for your children that speak the loudest to them. You love them or you wouldn't be trying to figure how to do this. Parents, I promise, your love is enough. *You* are enough. Your kids want honest, genuine conversation, not statistical data. Your kids don't need an expert to speak with them on matters of relationships. They need *you* to simply share openly, from your heart. *They need you to show them what healthy choices look like.*

WALKING THE TALK

Questions to Ponder

Hurdle Three addresses our concern for expertise in the area of intimacy and relationships. You are much more prepared for the task at hand than you might believe.

1. Currently, who talks/instructs your children on matters of intimacy and relationships? (This is a time to be honest. You cannot work on this area if you refused to admit what might be lacking.)
2. Do you feel "qualified" to speak to your children on intimate topics? If not, list some reasons why.
3. Remember a time as a parent that you felt woefully unprepared. How did you successfully navigate the parent hurdle? Did things turn out as badly as you thought they would?
4. Prepare your arsenal. Look up and make a list of a few Scripture verses you could use when talking to your children. Remember, it is not just about the physical act. Your talk should entail purity, respect, true beauty, kindness, wisdom, love, modesty and God's free gift of salvation. I've included a few of mine in *Walk It Out*. Regardless of your "expert" or "lay" knowledge, as believers we have a guidebook to help us. How much are you relying on God's Word to help on your parenting journey?
5. Take a moment and meditate on 2 Timothy 3:16 - *"All Scripture is God-breathed and is useful for teaching, rebuking, correcting and training in righteousness."*
6. After you have your scripture verses, meditate on this: Do your own personal relationships reflect what God has instructed for those that love Him (love, respect, obedience etc.)?

WALKING THE TALK

Walk It Out

Take a moment and see where others are in having "the talk" with their children. You might have learned last week that many are not engaged at all in the discussion. Encourage one another in this season. Be accountable to one another as well. Remember, you don't have to go through this journey alone.

Discuss for a few moments what makes a person qualified to talk about relationships? Does a Ph.D. make someone more qualified to teach your children? Is it time to drown out people's opinions about how you are to raise your children, and turn to God for *His* counsel?

Here are a few scripture verses I find helpful when talking to my children, along with why I chose them. What would you add?

1 Corinthians 6:18 *"Flee sexual immorality. Every sin that a man does is outside the body, but he who commits sexual immorality sins against his own body.....for you were bought at a price; therefore glorify God in your body and in your spirit, which are God's."*

Simply put, when we are believers, our bodies are no longer ours. We were bought by the blood of Christ and therefore are called to a higher standard. We are to no longer live according to our fleshly desires but instead to strive to live a God-driven life that reflects how much He means to us. If we mindlessly excuse our behaviors and do what we wish with our bodies, we are not honoring God. The Scripture could also be used to address drinking, smoking, and other ungodly behaviors.

Ephesians 4:17-18 *"And so I insist—and God backs me up on this—that there be no going along with the crowd, the empty-headed, mindless crowd. They've refused for so long to deal with God that they've lost touch not only with God but with reality itself."* (The Message)

Have you ever asked your child why they did something and get an "I dunno" shrug? We need to make sure our children understand the importance of thinking for themselves. When everyone else is having sex, drinking, or [fill in the blank], we don't want our children going mindlessly along with the crowd. We want our children to be thinkers and doers of God's Word. This requires us to help our children learn to think for themselves, and that means we give them responsibility in everyday life.

1 Samuel 16:7
"But the LORD said to Samuel, "Do not look at his appearance or at his physical stature, because I have refused him. For the LORD does not see as man sees; for man looks at the outward appearance, but the LORD looks at the heart."

God is not concerned with how we look. He is, however, concerned with our hearts. You can be the most outwardly beautiful person and still be ugly on the inside. Through love, wisdom, kindness, and purity, our prayer should be that our children's true beauty will shine.

Ephesians 4:32 *"Be kind to one another."* (ESV)

This verse can be used as a reminder that we are to treat others with kindness. Remember, we are teaching our children they have value and so do others. If they know they have value, kindness will be extended to those around them.

Proverbs 13:20 *"He who walks with the wise grows wise."* (NIV)

We all pray our children will be surrounded with godly counsel. When they walk with persons of integrity and wisdom, they will emulate that same integrity and wisdom. It goes along with a saying I once heard, "Show me your friends and I will show you your future."

Proverbs 20:11 *"Even small children are known by their actions, so is their conduct really pure and upright?" (NIV)*

Our children need to be known by their deeds and the actions of our children should be honoring to God. A child's actions, appearance or decisions should not cause confusion or doubt to their Christian testimony. It is also a great reminder that we are examples for the world to see. We want our children to show the world Jesus!

Chapter Three: What Is the Parent's Role?

I have a confession for you. When I first starting teaching and counseling, and even when I first started writing, I focused solely on the ramifications of sex. I focused on why young adults shouldn't do it, what could happen if they did, and why God didn't want them to. I could literally redirect almost any conversation back to why sex, outside of God's design, could be devastating.

"Oh so you watched television last night? Did you know over 60 percent of all television shows have sexually explicit content?" [2]

Not sure why, but I never got any raving applause from my young adults for my educational prowess. Mind blowing. The students in my youth group eventually gave me the nickname "sex-pert." Clever, huh? I wouldn't have minded the name if my words had fallen on listening, eager ears, but unfortunately my approach was failing.

At the time, I didn't realize I was so focused on the doom and gloom of sex. My heart was truly in the right place. I wanted young adults to be empowered to make better decisions than I had. I became pregnant with my daughter my senior year of college. In a nine-month span, I went from looking at law school to trying to figure out how I was going to finish my undergrad and take care of a baby. My boyfriend and I had barely been dating six months when we discovered I was pregnant. We were still trying to figure out where our relationship was going. It was a very difficult time for me and forced both of us to grow up quickly. By the grace of God and my stubborn streak, I didn't end up a statistic like most. I was able to finish school, pursue a masters, and have a great career and a successful marriage; but it has not been without struggle.

I didn't want others to have it hard like me. I still don't. I don't want to see my kids make decisions that will lead them down difficult roads. No parent wants to see their children struggle. The fear that our children might repeat our mistakes can drive our motives and prevent us from seeing the real issues. And sometimes we don't know what to do, so we do nothing.

I want you to see that it goes so much farther than just a talk about the physical. The conversation can be about sex, drugs, alcohol, or any other struggle as our kids learn to live in an ungodly culture. I want you to realize that you and I are raising young men and women to be healthy, God-focused individuals. We are not, on the other hand, just trying to corral or suppress a physical drive. I am not interested in trying to change my children's behaviors; I want their hearts to change. Without a heart change, all we have created are children that will modify behavior based on fear of some consequence.

Remember what I said about us being triune beings? You cannot address the physical without addressing the emotional and spiritual components. We can raise health-conscious children that are fully educated about the physical aspects of intimacy but still see them fail because we, as their instructor, are not demonstrating healthy emotional and spiritual components in our homes.

What I hope to achieve in the next few sections is for us to realize the importance of these three points in our daily lives:

- A life of purity is not only about sex. We are all called to be pure in our walk with Christ.
- Our identity is in Christ alone. We are created in God's image and this fact needs to be celebrated, remembered and demonstrated through us.

- Our relationships with one another should reflect our honor to God.

Let's take a look at what our roles can look like in our home. You might be surprised that your role isn't about how much information you give them, but about what you show them by your daily relationships.

WALKING THE TALK

Role One: Encourage Healthy Self-Esteem and Body Image

I am acutely aware of the frailty of a teenager's self-confidence. I have witnessed first-hand in the counseling room what happens when young girls and boys have a distorted view of themselves. They search for meaning and acceptance from the attention of others. They compromise their bodies, their spirits and their thoughts for the sake of fitting in and feeling wanted. With that knowledge, I try very hard to ensure my son and daughter have a positive self-image. Raising self-confident young adults in a world where their eyes are assaulted daily with advertisements of Photoshopped models, unrealistic body goals, and misleading definitions of male and female roles can prove difficult. Many of you are noticing that regardless of how much you tell your children they are enough just as they are, they still don't appear satisfied with being themselves.

Over the last few months, my preteen daughter constantly stands in front of a mirror, poking on her little belly and asking me if I think she needs to work out. My daughter regularly plays two fairly intense sports that require a lot of physical exertion. She couldn't be overweight if she wanted to, but for some reason she is very self-conscious about how "big" she is. It concerned me enough that I began asking the opinions of friends with daughters around her age. I got varying answers. Some said it was just a stage that all girls went through, while others made no mention of having issues with their daughters. I do believe that little girls hit a certain age and their focus shifts from playing in the dirt to playing in the makeup.

Then I discovered an alarming thing: sometimes the negative messages are not coming from a magazine or television screen, but from me.

So here is my confession. I don't always like myself and can be my worst critic. I have more freckles on my face than I care to count. I am really tall and secretly long to be like the other average height girls with their petite frames. There are a billion and one things I wish I could change about my appearance. My attitude can get catty, especially when I feel intimidated by others. Sometimes, I even try to make myself feel better by pointing out the flaws of those around me.

At the end of the day, nothing I say to make myself feel better changes a single thing, but it can have a lasting effect on those watching me, especially my daughter and son. Every time I put myself down, talk about others or try to be anything else than what God designed me to be I am not only hurting myself, I am also wounding my children.

Here are two ways parents can help their children develop a positive self-image. It might be different than you think. And it starts with us.

1. Develop your own positive self-image

We tell our children how precious they are, and in the same sentence we tear ourselves down. The message is contradictory and it is harming the very ones we love. All parents want their children to grow into confident young adults, and we need to remember our little ones learn from example. If all they hear you say about yourself or your spouse is negative, how are they to develop a positive self-image? How will they ever learn to embrace their spouses and others in their lives as they are? Parents, we must embrace ourselves as the beautiful creations of our Most High. Instead of shaming our differences, we need to learn that it is those very differences that make us beautiful.

We cannot tell our children that they should accept themselves or others when we don't accept ourselves.

Many of us parents think that self-esteem and a positive body image will come from playing sports, being the perfect size, or having all the right "stuff." We kill ourselves at a nine-to-five in the pursuit of a great fortune because we live in a society that tells us our success is our badge of honor. Our self-image is mistakenly rooted in the world and not in Christ. There is nothing wrong with having success or beauty, but I think we have lost sight that we are created in the image of our Maker and this is where our hope can be found. Scripture reminds us in Colossians 2:7: *"Let your roots grow down into HIM, and let your lives be built on HIM. Then your faith will grow strong in the truth you were taught, and you will overflow with thankfulness."* The truth of this passage has been lost in a world that focuses on everything else. When our roots are not in our Creator, we will find ourselves dissatisfied by who stares back at us in the mirror.

My question is this: Are you satisfied with yourself and your life? If you say no, don't expect your children to be. If your children are seeing you constantly striving for perfection with your body, in your job or with your status in life, don't be surprised to see a child that strives for that same worldly perfection. And when the world cannot give it to them, they will go searching for it in other people and relationships. I have watched the self-demoralizing of many teens in the counseling room too often to count. I have experienced it myself. When you do not realize the image in which you were made, you will devalue the very temple that God created so lovingly. Parents, help your children develop roots of self confidence in the only One Who can sustain and satisfy them.

Before we can build up our children, we need to provide that example to follow. When your children know that their bodies are precious and require care, they will be much more likely to protect them. Seeing their parents' confidence in themselves will provide that much needed example to follow.

WALKING THE TALK

2. Get your identity in Christ alone

1 Peter 2:9 reads *"But you are a chosen generation, a royal priesthood, a holy nation, His own special people, that you may proclaim the praises of him who called you out of darkness into his marvelous light."* Our children are looking for their places in this world. They will either find their identity in the world, which is fleeting, or in Christ. We need to constantly remind our children that the world's things will not fulfill nor define them. It is when we seek Christ and find our identity only in Him that we learn our true character.

Parents, we can buy them all the name brand clothes, enter them in every beauty contest in the world and still create a hollow shell of a person that has no idea who they are. *Feeling* good about oneself based on worldly possessions and accomplishments alone does not always mean they have a positive sense of worth. You see that I stressed the word feeling. So what do I mean?

If a child's identity is based on looking a certain way or having certain things, the image or possession will determine how they feel about themselves. If they achieve their goal, they will feel good about themselves. If they are struggling with a particular task, then their feelings can create a negative personification. We must watch how much weight we place on status.

Both of my kiddos play sports. We seem to have found our niche in the game of soccer. And though I am somewhat biased, both of my little athletes are good. Each of my children had the honor of playing in the soccer league championships last year. One of my soccer players came away as soccer league champion while the other experienced a crushing defeat in round two, ending their season in second place. At the end of the day, we were *all* exhausted and sunburned (SPF 50, you had one job and you blew it.)

WALKING THE TALK

If you want to see the true colors of parents and coaches, throw them on a soccer field and hold out a championship trophy for the taking. It gets interesting. We got front row seats, minus the popcorn. Coaches were making threats to other coaches. Parents were encouraging very un-sportsman like behavior. I am not sharing this to praise the awesome athletic abilities of my kiddos or shame parents that get a little over zealous at their kid's sporting events. I am, however, sharing a lesson that we can all stand to learn about trying to get our *identity* in life's circumstances.

After the pictures were taken and the medals were given, we went on with our normal, everyday lives. There was not an entourage of people lining the street where we live, applauding my soccer stars for their long hard fight. No "Eye of the Tiger" played as we walked into our home. First place kid went to their room and played video games. Second place kid went to their room and colored. My husband and I drank a gallon of Gatorade and collapsed on the couch, thankful the season was over. It was fun. It was exciting. At the end of the day, it was just a game.

We don't want children that are tossed to and fro based on their current situation or status. We want them anchored in truth and their identity fixed in Christ. Parents, we need that understanding as well. Our own identity is not to be placed on how much money we make or what we do for a career. Our identity does not stem from the square footage of our home or the cars parked in our driveway. As parents, we must be comfortable in our skin if we are to teach our children to be. Pointing them to their Creator will help them in their relationships as well. They won't seek out relationships to *feel* important, complete or loved. Their identity won't be based on how well they did in a sporting event or a beauty pageant. It will be rooted in Him, not fleeting emotions or circumstances. Galatians 5:16-24 reminds us, *"But I say, walk by the Spirit, and you will not gratify the desires of the flesh. For the desires of the flesh are against the Spirit, and the desires of the Spirit are against the flesh, for these are opposed to each other, to keep you from doing the things you want to do. But if you are led by the Spirit, you are not under the law. Now the works of the flesh are evident: sexual immorality, impurity, sensuality, idolatry, sorcery, enmity, strife, jealousy, fits of anger, rivalries, dissensions, divisions."(ESV)*

Our lives will have meaning and worth only when we serve God and find our identity in Him alone. My concern for the generations coming up is that this message is being lost in a sea of technology, status and empty worldly praise. No wonder we never seemed to be satisfied. Though I am very proud of my kids' accomplishments on the field, when we go home our family doesn't place medals over the value of their souls. I want them to be champions for a greater cause and that cause is Christ. It is through the identity they find in Christ that their self-image will be built and glorified.

WALKING THE TALK

Questions to Ponder

Are you starting to see how your role goes beyond just conversation? Our own identity and acceptance of God's truth about us can be uncomfortable to address but it is necessary. Your walk in truth will speak louder than any words you might say.

1. According to Webster's Dictionary, identity is defined as *"distinguished character."* As believers, how are we distinguished?
2. Why should we avoid relying on our feelings and thoughts when it comes to parenting? Let's take a look at what Scripture tells us. Read Jeremiah 17:9-10 and Proverbs 28:26.
3. When we are struggling with who we are, how can that lack of identity affect our daily lives?
4. Can social media play a role in how we view ourselves/children?
5. Have you been guilty of putting yourself down, or of being extremely focused on external beauty and success? Take a moment and lift your prayers to God, and ask Him to renew your heart for things of His beauty.

Walk It Out

Discuss how others define identity. Is our identity based on how we are feeling? Is our identity defined by our personal accomplishments, relationships, etc.? It is important for parents to understand that they and their children must find their self-worth in Christ alone and not in earthly endeavors and relationships. If a parent's identity is determined by the behavior, success or beauty of their children, they will feel like failures when the child fails. The same is true for our children. When external factors determined their identity, they will only feel worthy when things are going well.

Why is this important? When your children get in relationships, platonic or romantic, we want them to understand that another person (outside Christ) cannot complete them. Many times, a dating teen will become so obsessed with a relationship that nothing else matters. We want our children to balance their relationships in a healthy manner. When dating teens know that God is their focus, they are less likely to engage in activities that compromise their beliefs.

Look up "Who I Am in Christ" on the Freedom in Christ Ministries website (current link is https://www.ficm.org/handy-links/#!/who-i-am-in-christ). This is an excellent Scriptural reference on our secure identities in Christ. Discuss the versed you struggle to believe. Share this with your children.

Have someone read Jeremiah 17:9 and Proverbs 28:26. Following our hearts can be dangerous if we are not studiously studying God's Word. As parents, we want our children to be grounded in truth. If we, as parents, are fickle with emotions, our children will learn and imitate that trait. It can be a larger concern when our teens begin dating or start making important life decisions. We want our children to decide their path based on God's will and not on how they feel at the time. *Identity* is found in Christ alone!

Take a few moments to discuss the effects on our families when everything is projected on social media. How can that affect you and your children? Think of how you can limit that outside source.

Role Two: Model Healthy Relationships

I am an advocate of a two-parent home largely because I was not part of one. My mother and father divorced when I was little and my mother did not remarry. I don't blame her for choosing to stay single. She dealt with a lot of emotional abuse that would last her a lifetime. In some sense, I believe she wanted to protect us from another potentially "bad" relationship.

I could write a book just on the effects of divorce on children, but this isn't the place for that discussion. I am simply sharing some history about my own family because I feel that I missed out on some valuable lessons about positive, God-centered relationships. Now, many years later, with a family of my own, I am hyper aware of my own family dynamics. My husband and I work hard in our marriage for one another, and we also allow our children to see the good, the bad, and the ugly.

Many of my friends have told me they have never seen their parents fight, nor have they overheard decisions on family financial matters being made. At one time, I thought that was how I would handle my own family matters, but it just didn't work for us. My husband and I want our children to be aware of what it takes to actually make a marriage work day-to-day. I want them to understand it's not always about the glass slipper, but the daily grind.

Our marriages should reflect the covenant we have with God. It is through relationships that God is truly mirrored. It is through our marriage union that we experience how to exemplify the love of Christ in our day-to-day lives. Our children need to see this partnership unfolding so they understand what a healthy relationship truly is.

Now before I lose those who are single parents, I understand that a two-parent home may not be how your specific situation turned out. Our reality may not be the fairytale life we'd hoped to experience. As I have already stated, I grew up in a divorced home. I understand how a single-parent home functions differently from that of a two-parent home. With that understanding, I will write the next few sentences as respectfully as I can. Being a single parent – divorced, separated, or never married – is not a free pass to avoid the hard topic of relationships. You are still called to be a God-fearing example to your children. It might look different than a family with a mom and a dad, but you are still called to exemplify Christ in your home. The covenant was always with God. Your relationships serve as the visual.

So what does "exemplifying Christ" mean for you as a single parent?

1. **Remain pure.**

God does not mix words on the matter of intimacy. 1 Thessalonians 4:3 states, *"For this is the will of God, your sanctifications that you should abstain from sexual immorality."* The scripture verses warning us against sexual immorality were not written just for hormone-driven teenagers. Nowhere in Scripture does it give a different set of standards for adults. God is very clear that if you are not married, you are to remain sexually abstinent. If you are going to ask your teen to remain free from sexual sin, shouldn't you? We can tell our children all day to *"do what I say, not what I do,"* but it has very little staying power. Remember, children learn from example. You have to walk the talk.

I have a dear friend who divorced when her daughter was just a few years old. For the longest time, she did not date. As her daughter was reaching her teen years, my friend met a fine Christian man and they began dating. He also had a daughter. From the very beginning, they made the decision to remain sexually pure until they were married. They even went to their teenage daughters and shared their decision with them. My friend told me that they knew they could not ask their teenagers to do something they were not willing to do. They lived out their commitment in front of their children. Do you think their commitment left a lasting impression on those two teenage girls? You bet it did! Their daughters learned a real lesson that was lived out in the relationship choices of their parents.

Please hear me out. First of all, if you are a single parent, I know it's hard and it can be lonely; I watched my mother struggle financially, emotionally, and spiritually for years. It's hard to keep God's standard for purity – abstinence – in a culture where physical relationships are used as a relief from the pain of brokenness. I have several friends who are divorced, and it breaks my heart to see how they live. They jump into dating relationships, introducing their children to men/women that may not even be a part of their life next week. All these relationships that you are in and out of are confusing to your children and more damaging to you all than you realize. May I also remind you that in the broken world we live in, you could easily be putting yourself and your children in danger.

Next, please allow me to be blunt with you: *you can't play house.* I cannot tell you how many divorced professing believers I have watched do this, and how it has led them away from God and toward a life full of struggle and compromise. You cannot live a lifestyle that is contradictory to God's design and expect to have it function properly, or expect to have His blessing and approval. I had a friend tell me one time that she wanted her live-in boyfriend to show some spiritual leadership with her children so she knew how he would lead when they got married. I had to be the bearer of bad news and tell her that first, it was not his responsibility to lead because he was not her husband, and second, her relationship that included sex outside marriage was not God-honoring.

WALKING THE TALK

My intent in sharing this is not to bring condemnation to you if you are in an ungodly relationship right now, but to speak truth that the Holy Spirit can use to bring conviction. Remember that conviction sheds light on what is right and what is wrong, and allows God to reach down and say, "Come to me... and I will forgive you." Conviction points to the solution through the blood of Christ. It is never too late to receive God's forgiveness. Ending an ungodly relationship is very hard, but He'll help you every step of the way. In the long run, you'll be glad you did.

2. Pursue Christ

Single parents need to focus their time on getting to know their First Love again and on sharing that love with their children, not looking for a mate. Your relationship with your Heavenly Father needs to be cultivated above all else. Matthew 6:33 tells us to seek first the kingdom of God and His righteousness. In this season of singleness, we need to show our children that our fulfillment comes from Christ and not man. There is nothing wrong with wanting to be married, but it is by growing in Christ that we are healed and made whole. Wholeness doesn't come from our human relationships. A dear friend of mine who has never been married expressed her struggles with her singleness. It wasn't until her early thirties that she looked around and realized "everyone" was married and starting families. Of course, she felt pressure to have a diamond on her left hand and to one day hold babies on her lap. Instead of pursuing those things as her focus, she prayed for God to make Himself known to her like never before. She prayed for contentment that can only come from Him. After she said that prayer, she began pursuing Christ in her everyday life. I was so moved by the prayers she shared with me. She later told me she had fallen in love with God all over again. How beautiful!

WALKING THE TALK

As I mentioned, I know that it can be hard as a single parent because of how my mom struggled, and from counseling single parents and their children. My prayer for any family would be that they never have to experience divorce or death of a partner, but in a broken world created by sin, broken families will happen. Regardless of your role in that brokenness, we must remember we can still show our children the most important relationship they have is with God. When your relationship with Christ is strong, your heart will pursue relationships that are God honoring. Single parents, you still have an important role to demonstrate to your children. God can use you mightily, if you are willing to do things His way.

Bottom line: in our thoughts, in our prayers and in our parenting, we need to pursue God's will and not our own.

Married couples must do the same. So how do you pursue Christ in your marriage, remain pure and set the example for your children? Glad you asked!

1. Pray together

1 Thessalonians 5:17 states we should pray without ceasing. For me, this one was the hardest. Religion might have been woven in my childhood somewhere, but I don't ever recall praying as a family. Prayer was always addressed as something you did in your personal time with God. So praying together as a couple and as a family was a little odd at first. (Not for the kids, but for us.) Desiring our family to have a prayer time together, we started at dinner with my husband leading. Slowly, the kids started praying around the table. Now, it's not uncommon for the kids to see us, as a couple, praying over the smallest matters. Before big

WALKING THE TALK

decisions are made, the kids know we will pray about them first.

If you want your kids to have a desire for God, they need to see a genuine desire for Him in your relationships with Him and each other.

And I can tell you firsthand that it can do wonders for your marriage when you share such intimate times. If praying is new to you, start with mealtime, then let it grow to bedtime prayers. Before you know it, you are talking with God about everything. There is nothing wrong with starting in small ways. Just start praying together and watch how God will work.

2. Know Your Role

"We want our husbands to lead, but we want it to be our way."

The first time I heard another woman say this was in a Bible study. She shared that after one failed marriage, she had learned a vital point that she was employing in her second marriage: to let her man lead the way he was called.

The biggest complaint I hear from other women is that their men won't lead the family, be it in the area of discipline, finances, or spiritual. I, too, have made those same complaints, but when I pull back the veil of truth, I see that many times my husband couldn't lead because I was in the way.

We wives want a man to lead as long as it's the way *we* would lead. We want our husbands to be the spiritual leaders of the home, but only when it goes with what we want. We want our husbands to discipline the children, until we think he is being too tough on them. *Bluntly put, women like the* idea *of being led, but not the* reality. Marriage is give and take, and sometimes you have to give more than you get back. But if all you do is fight your husband on every leadership decision he makes, expect him to eventually stop leading. In some sad cases, the husband will never again step up to the plate.

Just as the wife has an ordained role in her family, God has also called the husband into a specific marriage role and that role should bring honor and respect to God. A man can be a strong leader but gentle with his family as he leads them. Men are called to honor and respect their wives and the leadership role bestowed to them should not be taken advantage of. 1 Peter 3:7 (NIV) states, *"Husbands, in the same way be considerate as you live with your wives, and treat them with respect as the weaker partner and as heirs with you of the gracious gift of life, so that nothing will hinder your prayers."*

For too long, we have bought into society's lie that a man can only lead his home with an iron fist, and for a woman to submit to her husband's authority, she must forfeit her opinions, honor, and dignity. There is nothing further from the truth. Look around you. Do you see how distorted the roles are of a man and woman? Do you see couples happier? I see stressed women give up precious time with their families to climb the corporate ladder, and sometimes carry that business drive into their home and take over. I see complacent men that no longer have the drive to fight and provide for their families – they are not leading.

Without God, I see confusion. I see loss of perspective, respect, and love. I am not saying each family will look exactly the same, nor am I advocating that women should not work. What I am saying is this: if God is not your family's focus, and the head of the home is not your husband, then your family/marriage is out of order.

I was interviewed by a writer once who asked me if I ever felt unappreciated in my marriage. She was surprised when I replied with an unhesitant no. The interviewer asked me to expound on what I meant. I've learned the role that God has called me to as a wife and a mother. Many of us do not understand fully how God made us to complement our spouses, and this misunderstanding is why seeds of discontent are sowed. As unpopular as this might be, even among Christians, women were never meant to lead their homes or their families. Men were created to be the leaders, providers, and protectors of the home. Women are to be a help mate to their spouse, taking care of the home and the children. Over the years, as the glass ceiling has lifted and women have gained equality, women have been made to believe that if they choose a more traditional role, they are somehow less of a woman. Men have been accused of being chauvinist, trying to oppress their women, if they take the role of leader in their families. These are both lies. Our roles as a wife/mother and husband/father can be some of the hardest roles we play in our life, but the rewards that come with understanding and functioning in our correct place is beyond wonderful. Families have direction, marriages have leadership, and God remains at the center of our relationships.

3. Make decisions together

Children should see their parents consulting one another before making small or big decisions. There is nothing wrong with a couple disagreeing on what the best decision for the family might be. The point for our children is not to see who wins. The point is to show them that even in times when we disagree we can find a solution and honor each other in the process. Allowing our children to see us making decisions *together* will not only show them how to be a decision maker, but it is a great chance to emulate a healthy relationship model to our children.

Decision making should never be one sided. And believe it or not, it's truly okay for our children to see us at times where we just don't like one another very much. I do not mean physical confrontation or angry outbursts where we are directing profanity or insults towards each other. *Abuse of any kind is never acceptable.* But there is no reason to believe our kids will be in therapy if they see mom and dad disagree with each other. In fact, disagreeing is a chance to let your kids see how to handle conflict respectfully and maturely. It is also a chance for them to see that a real man leads with dignity and not brute strength, and a gentle woman can speak up without being disrespectful or rude.

Decision making is not always about how respectful you are when disagreeing. It can also be a chance for your children to see what healthy decision making can look like in action. Seeing that financial issues are a large factor in the divorce rate, I want to encourage each of you, as a couple, to strive to show how being good decision makers will also help you be better stewards of what you have been given. I see problems in this area too often to recount. A couple gets along in every aspect of their marriage except when it comes to the green in their bank accounts (or lack thereof). Of course, money is not everything in a marriage, but knowing that the light bill is paid and the bank won't default on the home mortgage prevents a lot of stress. We all want our children to have relationships that are healthy and we want to raise our children to understand the importance of being responsible. Part of ensuring that is making sure our decisions reflect that idea in our day-to–day dealings with finances.

When our children see us work things out in partnership instead of two individuals trying to get their own way, they understand that healthy relationships take work. More importantly, they understand what it means to value one another. Philippians 2:2-5 says it beautifully, *"Make my joy complete by being like-minded, having the same love, being one in spirit and of one mind. Do nothing out of selfish ambition or vain conceit. Rather, in humility value others above yourselves, not looking to your own*

WALKING THE TALK

interests but each of you to the interests of the others. In your relationships with one another, have the same mindset as Christ Jesus..."

4. Stay pure together

This might look a little different than purity as a single parent. The importance of purity in your marriage should still be a top priority. We should protect our marriages from external and internal dangers. First, I believe that children need to know that even after they are married, they still must pursue their spouse. Our children laugh and cover their eyes when they see my husband and I kiss, but there is a look of contentment on their faces too. They know we love each other because we show it not only in our speech, but in our actions. Scripture instructs us on matters of intimacy with our spouses. 1 Corinthians 7:2 states, *"Nevertheless, because of sexual immorality, let each man have his own wife, and each woman with her own husband."*

Next, sex can be used as a connector or a demolisher in marriage. When we connect in a giving sexual union, remember that it's not just physical, but mental, emotional, and spiritual as well. Sex is meant to be shared between husband and wife, bringing them closer to one another, not just to a goal. Sex is necessary for a healthy marriage. It is not something our spouses should get to share in just when they have *earned* it. Please do not manipulate such a beautiful intimate time. When couples are connected, physically, mentally, emotionally and spiritually, the marriage roles will easily fall into place without the coercion, the complaining or the dictating. Try it and see how much better your relationship with your spouse gets.

When sex is "used" in a selfish way it can become a demolisher. Marriage is deprived of intimacy and we can turn to fillers. In some cases, porn defiles the marriage bed.

WALKING THE TALK

In other cases, marriages are destroyed because of extramarital affairs. Not only does this affect you, but it will greatly influence the relationships of your children.

I am sure many of you are like me. I want my kids to see that my husband and I love one another. I want to demonstrate that by the manner in which we emotionally, spiritually, and physically provide for one another. By nurturing our intimacy and letting our children see us demonstrating affection in our day-to-day marriage, we are showing our children that our family is here to stay.... through the good, the bad, and the ugly.

Questions to Ponder

How are you doing in your relationships? For many, being honest about where you are in your marriage – or your singleness – will be hard. It can be especially uncomfortable to share in a group setting. Let me encourage you to be bold, be transparent. Your openness might be exactly what someone else needs right now.

1. How do our own relationships reflect God's covenant with us?
2. Where does your faith, family, and focus line up on the priority list? Do your priorities line up biblically?
3. Take a look at Song of Solomon 2:15. What little foxes could ruin the vineyards of our marriages?
4. If you are married, are there areas in your relationship with your spouse that need to be mended by God? Remember, you are a team. Allow God to strengthen your relationship by drawing near to Him.
5. If you are single, are you pursuing relief from your loneliness through sinful relationships? Remember that only God can make you whole, heal your brokenness, and give you the peace you are seeking. Ask Him for help to leave behind anything, or anyone, that can lead you away from Him.

Walk It Out

You and I, and **every believer**, were created to live in marital union with God, both now and in the age to come. Our covenant is with Him. Everything about a healthy marital union on this earth has been designed by God to be a reflection of the union we are meant to have with God:

Earthly Union	Godly Union
Our marriage covenant binds us together until death	God's covenant with His people is forever (Psalm 105:8)
Our wedding celebration / rings are a declaration of our covenant to one another	Our public declaration and baptism declare our covenant with God (Colossians 2:12-13)
Shared intimate moments – sexual, emotional, spiritual –resulting in a oneness	As intimacy grows with God, we begin thinking and reflecting more Christ-like characteristics (Romans 8:29)

WALKING THE TALK

Discuss these parallels. Can you think of more parallels between earthly unions and godly unions?

What if you are single: does this look different? In 1 Corinthians 7:7, the Apostle Paul exhorts he wishes all people were single like him, thought it was a concession and not a commandment. *"I wish all men were [single] as I am. But each man has his own gift from God; one has this gift, another has that"* If you are single, for whatever reason, do not think for a second you have been excluded. As already stated, every believer, single or married, is created to live in a marital union with God. How you live while single can point others to God, and can grow and strengthen your own union with the Bridegroom.

Have you given your marriage/singleness to God? How can the little foxes of the vineyard, for both married and single, hinder your own walk? Sometimes it is not the big things that cause us to stumble in our relationships. Good intentions, lack of communication, expectations, and priorities can easily hinder our relationships with others and God. Talk it out, find accountability, and encourage one another.

WALKING THE TALK

Chapter Four: Age to Age

I believe in starting the discussion about healthy choices with our children when they are young. The one thing I have always advocated in sex education in the schools, churches and the homes is the need to start earlier than high school. Many kids by fourth and fifth grade have already learned information about sex from the school yard, regardless if only half of it is reliable. Many times, I think we, as parents, struggle with talking to our younger children because we are concerned that we might start them thinking about sex too young. Our silence can be driven by fear and lack of knowing what to tell them. By the time they get to the "appropriate" age to discuss intimacy and healthy relationships, we have lost valuable time and ground. No longer does a little, wide-eyed child stand looking up to you, hanging on your every word, but you are facing someone at eye level who thinks of themselves as a young adult, with their own opinions, perceptions, and feelings.

Unfortunately, we did not take the "start young" approach with our daughter. It was because of an incident at school that we finally realized it had to be us directing the intimacy conversation if we wanted her to have a solid Biblical foundation in making future choices. In this section, we will discuss how to handle that initial dialogue with calmness and grace.

Parents, sometimes it is a trial and error effort. I wish I had the knowledge years ago and understood the importance of starting young, but I didn't. If you are where I was with older children, please understand it is never too late. Start where you are. I have personally apologized to my daughter for taking such a passive stand with her in these matters. It is okay to admit that you wish you had done something differently. Your child will respect your honesty.

WALKING THE TALK

Though this chapter will not be exhaustive, I want to address a few things we should remember when talking to our children, youngest to oldest. The goal for each of the sections in this chapter can best be described as the following:

Preschoolers:
1. Learn the importance of using proper names for our body parts, and praising how God designed us differently as male and female
2. Respect the sanctity and beauty of human life

Grade School/Middle School:
1. Appreciate the beauty of puberty
2. Understand why modesty is important

High School:
1. Your teenager: a budding adult
2. Boundaries in relationships and social media
3. CPR Listening Skills

But before we go any further, I think it is good to address a few rules when engaging in conversation with your child. They might seem like obvious things, but too often cues are missed because we don't follow a few ground rules. As your child matures, the dialogue can get strained if you aren't careful. At this stage of the game, your mannerisms and stance are just as important as what you are saying. The words must not change, but your approach might need some fine tuning. I'd like to take a moment to address a few "rules" I find important when talking to a child of any age.

Rule #1: Let them talk

Earlier I mentioned a particular school incident with my daughter that made me realize it was time to start talking to her about sex. She was in second grade at a public school and came home talking about a conversation she overheard on the playground. A few of the fourth graders were talking about having sex when they "grew up." At this point, I had already been in the counseling room a little over two years and had learned how important it was to just listen. My daughter was talking, without any prompting from me, so I let her talk as I continued putting up dishes. My stance was very laid back. I didn't stop what I was doing when she began talking. Remember, you want the conversation to be a typical, normal, everyday dialogue.

Parents, when our children start school, we are no longer the only influencers in their lives. We are still the most important, though, so we can't forget it. As parents, we want to actively listen not just so we can respond, but so we can learn. In order for us to learn what is happening with our children, we need to become comfortable in playing a silent role and just listening to them. Sometimes the worst thing parents can do is open their mouths at the wrong time.

Rule #2: Eye contact is not mandatory

After two years in the counseling room, I found myself struggling with how my client listened, or in my observation, didn't listen. Young person after young person would enter the counseling room and immediately look at their phones. In fact, they would look everywhere but into my eyes. *How rude,* I thought, *I am trying to help them and they aren't even listening to me!* This is what the counseling room taught me: A teen doesn't have to be staring into your eyes to actually be listening. They hear you loud and clear.

WALKING THE TALK

If I have not learned anything else from working with young adults, I've learned that indirect eye contact does not indicate guilt or lack of interest. When your children are fidgeting with their phones, playing with a toy or looking out the window as you are discussing an issue with them, don't think they are not listening. Many times, they are. Believe me when I say, children (especially older children) can multi-task like a ninja. They are using their phone and/or their surroundings, in many cases, to buffer. In some cases this is not acceptable, but in the case of the dreaded "talk" I think it can alleviate stress and embarrassment.

Long discussions during a drive are a great place to start talking. Your eyes are on the road and not on them. Your child might not feel as much like they are being interrogated. Formality is not always the best rule of thumb. Picture this: Your mom and dad walk into your bedroom, hovering over you as you sit on the side of your twin bed, nervous and already on edge from what they will say. All eyes are on you. Would you feel open to talk?

Rule #3: Don't be so quick to share your thoughts

Another hindrance of a well-meaning parent is they tend to jump in and dominate the conversation. Silence freaks us parents out. Think about the example of my daughter. Though my facial expressions were calm, my heart was rapidly beating, threatening to leap from my chest. After my daughter finished telling me about the playground conversation, I leaned back against the counter and very nonchalantly (on the outside) asked her, *"Well, what do you think about what they said?"*

While she continued to play at the counter, she shrugged her little shoulders and replied, *"I guess if you love someone enough and you're old enough, it's okay."* Parents, this was from the mouth of a babe, my eight-year-old babe. The playground conversation I just shared is happening, even in second grade, so we need to be ready to address it. Now, the raging panic inside my head in light of my daughter's response could have easily taken over. Parents, it is during conversational turns such as this that we must be careful not to let a vomit of words spill out. While I cringed on the inside and wanted to automatically tell her she was wrong and that God designed sex for marriage, I didn't.

Instead, I responded, *"So what age is appropriate for having sex?"* Children will let you know where they are on the subject if you can just keep your cool. From my daughter's response, I observed we needed to spend more time explaining God's design for sex. I hope you see that they are never too young to start talking but we must handle it properly or the door of opportunity will slam in our faces.

The conversation might not even take off at that point, but let the message marinate. Be prepared to come back and address the issue after they have processed it. Don't nag! Ask your child one time if they have questions but always leave the conversational door open with them. Tell them that you want them to come to you with questions. In turn, parents, you must be willing to just listen when they do. Jumping in the conversation before your child has a chance to ask anything or process it will end the conversation before you can blink. Don't do it! Mum is the word.

Gather information from your kids, parents. Ask questions. Refrain from preaching. Hear what your child is saying and gently guide the conversation. You've got this.

WALKING THE TALK

Preschoolers (2s-5s)

The great thing about starting the conversation in the early years is you have plenty of time to practice the dialogue. The conversation can begin slowly. With preschool age children, you are just starting the basic dialogue on body image and God's beautiful design: *them.* It is a time to really praise the Creator and the beauty of His creations. Very few children at this age are going to ask for a lot of detail. With preschoolers, everyday life situations will help aid you in creating dialogue. Trust me when I say they will always provide you with a chance to answer questions.

I am sure as a parent you know that privacy is a luxury we do not have. At some point, your child has probably barged into the bathroom when you were showering. When my little boy was three he walked into the bathroom just as my husband was exiting the shower. With big eyes, my little boy asked, *"Daddy, why is your peepee so big?"* I was in the master bedroom that is connected to our bath and happen to overhear my son's question. I could not help but chuckle. I could almost see the crimson color creeping up my husband's face as my son stood in awe. I knew what we needed to address just from those few moments. See, your child will always provide the opportunity for dialogue at the most inopportune times.

What topic could we have discussed with such a question, you ask?

The difference between male and female

Children should know the proper names for their body parts. I know most parents have nicknames for their children's private areas. Though it might be more comfortable calling their privates areas "tutu" or "peepee" you really should avoid it as much as you can. Girls need to know they have a vagina and boys need to know they have a penis. My son presented the opportunity for us to address that vital first step. My husband, once clothed, went to my son and explained that though he was not in trouble, he needed to knock on the door before coming into the bathroom. He then continued to explain to our son that though there is nothing wrong with our body parts, they are not there for public display. It was also an intro lesson to modesty – yes, even boys need that talk. Finally, my husband explained the importance of knowing the proper names for our body parts. Daddy did not have a "peepee" but a penis, just as our son did.

With the discussion of body parts, my son wanted to know why God made boys and girls different. As parents, we should tell them that God designed male and female bodies to function differently, but both play a very important role in creating new life. I can't help but share a story I heard the other day from a parent. Her husband was trying to explain how the body parts function together. My friend told me her husband used a pencil and an eraser top to explain the "mechanics" of sexual intercourse. I can assure you that image will never be *erased* from the child's memory (pun intended).

In my opinion, the "how" of sex is not as important at this age as fostering respect for one's body. Sex is a natural thing for people, so the how will be a natural progression for them. The mechanics will come later. Right now we want to make sure they understand that they are created in the image of God and we are His beautiful creations. When we can help our children understand how special they are and the awesome role God designed them for, they will learn to respect themselves. When we know that something has value, we will cherish and protect it.

> *"For You formed my inward parts; You covered me in my mother's womb. I will praise You, for I am fearfully*

WALKING THE TALK

and wonderfully made; marvelous are Your works and that my soul knows well. My frame was not hidden from You, when I was made in secret, and skillfully wrought in the lowest parts of the earth. Your eyes saw my substance, being yet unformed, and in Your book they all were written, the days fashioned for me, when as yet there were none of them" (Psalm 139:13-16)

Now that we've shared with our children the real names for their body parts, the next topic we'll undoubtedly face is about babies. Where do they come from and how will they get out? This becomes even more urgent if you are expecting a child, or if you have a friend or relative sporting a growing belly. It's not necessary to get too much into the weeds at this age, but be honest with your child that the gift of life is from God.

How will the baby get out?

Now that your child understands they have a special role in the creation of life, they may ask you how the baby will get out once it gets in. I will share a personal account with you. There is a three year age difference between my daughter and son. As my belly grew with each passing day in my second pregnancy, my daughter's curiosity got the best of her. She would raise my shirt and get really close to my belly button. When I asked what she was doing, she told me she was looking for how her brother would get out of my belly.

As I shared earlier, the talk did not start immediately with our daughter. I don't think my husband or I ever really thought about the importance of starting at this age. Though I cannot recall the exact words I used, I am sure I did not handle it the proper way. I remember something about storks...see, I have the same mishaps and regrets; I hope you can learn from them.

Parents, we need to be clear when we talk to our children. Our answers might make sense to us, but depending on the age and maturity of our children, it may not be so clear to them. Directness is important. Avoid vague answers that will allow your small one to believe something was implied when it wasn't. Matter-of-fact answers will suffice, and will satisfy their curiosity. If your child asks how the baby will get out, tell them that (in most cases) the baby will come out through your vagina. Avoid the stork talks or other vague analogies. Point to the Creator and how He made us this way. Don't give credit for the beauty of delivering human life to a fairytale.

It's not awkward unless you make it awkward. Only you can judge the readiness of your children, but in most cases when the question of "how did the baby get in there?" arises, offer a very simple but straightforward explanation. You can talk about how a mother makes a tiny egg inside her body every month, and daddy's special seed will join with mommy's egg at the right time to create a new life. This is a great time to teach about the importance and sanctity of human life.

Questions to Ponder

We only scratched the surface of what to say to your preschooler about sex, but hopefully you see the importance of your role in this matter. Most importantly, I hope you see, after pondering the questions below, that it goes beyond the mentioning of body parts and their names.

1. Why is it important for your children to grasp the difference between male and female? Are we just talking about body parts, or does this topic go deeper?

2. What are your <u>opinions</u> of the role of male and female? It is important to recognize where you stand on this issue, for it will greatly affect how you raise your children. (Later we will discuss how our opinions line up with Scripture).

3. Take time to read and meditate on these passages:

    Ephesians 5:22-24
    Colossians 3:18
    1 Corinthians 11:3
    1 Peter 3:7
    Ephesians 5:25

4. Do you agree, in your heart, with what Scripture tells us are the roles of male and female? Are God's commands for our families always easy to follow?

WALKING THE TALK

Walk It Out

I want to go a little deeper in the talking points to address some of the current issues we, as a society, are facing. I hope you understand that our talks go way beyond the names of our body parts, or if storks have a place in the discussion. I hope that you will take a moment and discuss why parents must teach their children, often by example, the proper roles of men and women, both in the workplace and in the home. I find it relevant to this topic, and absolutely necessary, that each of us be completely honest about what we believe. God has worked drastically in this area of my life. For a long time, I struggled with the idea of submission, and with what I believed to be a very subservient role of a wife and mother.

In little more than half a century, American culture has experienced a massive restructuring of values. Our moral and spiritual standards are completely confused. One of the reasons for the confusion lies with the erosion and alteration of gender roles.

Women no longer understand or find honor in their role as a wife and mother. Men are no longer the spiritual leaders of the home or the providers for their families. Homosexuality is considered normal in our culture, and same sex couples are demanding that their lifestyle not only be accepted, but be celebrated. Let me stress this to you: I understand the sensitivity of this topic, I have family members that live alternative lifestyles. Many of you do as well, and you probably feel the internal struggle between what is right and what is merciful.

Not everything God says in His word will give you or anyone else the warm fuzzies. God's Word convicts, and it offends. We are called to be truth speakers, all while extending a hand of love to the lost. God's Word will not be popular or easy to share at times, but if we, as believers, believe that the Word is God-breathed and useful for teaching, rebuking, correcting and training (2 Timothy

3:16) then we must hold to that truth, even when it offends us and requires changes in our relationships or lifestyles. This is a good time to reflect on the verses provided in question #3. Are we teaching our children what God's word says on the roles of men and women, or are we teaching them the roles suggested by man? God did not make a mistake in how He created us. He made both roles – male and female – important and unique.

Grade School and Middle School

I blinked and it happened. The change was upon us like a snap of the fingers. One day, my little girl is short and still has her baby fat. Then, in one turn of the head, a young lady emerges from her cocoon, tall and absolutely breathtaking.

Sometimes it is hard to grasp. Where did my baby go? One day we are shopping for Dora the Explorer pajamas, the next day we are looking at bras. Then I look at her younger brother and realize in a very short span of time, his voice will begin to change and the blond hair on his legs will gradually darken. I often wonder if I am ready for this. I have to remind myself to breathe. Inhale. Exhale.

Many of you are there right now - we can share a box of tissues. Even as I write this, I fight the urge to cry. Thank goodness for two ply. It is such a beautiful time in our children's lives and we need to remember to celebrate the changes. This season of life we call puberty can be stressful on them. Their emotions are all over the place. I am sure many of you have watched your overly emotional, sensitive offspring and thought *"Who is this?"*

There are several points during this time of change we need to remember and discuss with our grade and middle schoolers.

Puberty is a beautiful time in adolescence

Psalms 139:14 says it best: *"I praise you because I am fearfully and wonderfully made; your works are wonderful, I know that full well."* I will address this point first from a woman's perspective simply because, well, I am a woman. Let's talk about periods – not the punctuation, but the menses. It is very easy to see this time as more of a curse than a blessing. How we approach the topic of periods will either help our girls get through this time of change or make it harder.

When I got my period, I felt like I had been dealt a death sentence. It was embarrassing, and from the responses I heard from other women around me, periods were a horrible thing to have. I know it might sound odd, but we need to celebrate this rite of passage into womanhood. Try not to make negative comments about having a period. Avoid statements like the following:

> *"Poor thing, you got your period. I'm so sorry."*
> *"Men have it so much easier than women- they don't have periods."*
> *"I hate being a girl. Periods are the worst."*

Instead of showing pity for our daughters, let's remind them that having a period is a great honor. It is our body's way of letting us know we are women, able to create life. Yes, periods can be hard and uncomfortable, but we are fearfully and wonderfully made and that includes our menstrual cycle. During puberty, our bodies are changing and are being prepared for what they were made to do. I have not always thought like this, but how awesome it is that God designed us to be able to create and carry life, and then to be able to feed our young with the milk of our breasts. Wow! That would not be possible without the stages of puberty, including menses. Let's celebrate it, not dread it.

Let's not forget the guys. Boys might not have periods, but they experience their own rite of passage into manhood. Their voices deepen, body hair darkens and the curvature of their limbs becomes more defined. They, too, can now contribute to the creation of life. It is very easy during this time and in our culture to send a different message to the boys. Parents, our sons need to understand the rite of passage into manhood does not involve the sexual exploitation of women. This time is not a chance to "sow their wild oats" but to learn what being a man truly is. 1 Timothy 4:12 states: *"Let no one despise you for your youth, but set the believers an example in speech, in conduct, in love, in faith, in purity"*. Sadly, in this society many boys and girls do not have the dual role models they need in their homes; but with or without two godly parent figures, we can teach them what a godly man and woman looks like because we have God's Word.

Neither my husband nor I had father figures in the home. We were both, however, very blessed to have grandparents and other godly influences in our lives. I have already mentioned that I became pregnant with my daughter my senior year of college. Simply put, I was not ready to be a mom. I was scared and very confused. When I told my boyfriend (now husband) that I was pregnant, he stepped up to the plate and took responsibility. At the beginning, I did not want to continue my pregnancy. I gave my boyfriend a pretty significant "out." All he had to do was help me get the funds to have an abortion. I can still see his face as I told him my plans. Laying his hands on my belly, he sobbed and pleaded with me on behalf of our child. *"I will raise her alone, Sarah,"* he told me. *"You can go back to school and finish and I won't ask anything of you. Our child deserves to live."* My boyfriend stepped up and became the man I needed. Because of that, a life was spared and a family was strengthened. I literally owe my daughter's life to him. I am a very blessed woman.

By telling you this part of my story, I hope you see that we can all step up and be the men and women we were called to be. No excuse is good enough; no struggles we face or parental absences in life could possibly stop God's will for us when we choose His ways. Remember that.

We must teach our children that even in times where they mess up or fall short, they still must take responsibility, and God will always help them through whatever they face. How can we expect them to grow up and be the men and women they were designed to be unless they are taught from God's Word and see examples of Christ-like decisions lived out before them in our life choices?

Modesty is important

As puberty begins, our children's bodies start changing and they can feel awkward. Some children are developing at warp speed while others are going through a more gradual change. I can recall coming back from summer break my sixth grade year and all my girlfriends having breasts while I was barely in a training bra. It was hard on my self-confidence. My girlfriends' drastic body changes brought attention from the boys and I realized that no one was looking at me. Several of my friends realized that their "new look" brought attention and they liked it.

This is a time we must be ready to explain to our children that we have a duty to protect one another. Deuteronomy 22:8 says, *"When you build a new house, you shall make a parapet for your roof, that you may not bring the guilt of blood upon your house, if anyone should fall from it."*

A parapet is a defensive mini-wall used as a means to protect. You can look at is as a type of security measure. This illustration can be used in the discussion of modesty as well. We don't dress to draw attention to our new bodies, not because there is something wrong with our bodies, but because we want to help protect the thoughts of our fellow neighbors - especially those dealing with their own changing bodies and feelings. In other words, we want to encourage our children to help protect their fellow believers from the temptation of lust. Will it always work? No, but as Christians we do have a duty to lift one another and to attempt to keep each other from stumbling. Romans 14:13

states, *"Therefore let us stop passing judgment on one another. Instead, make up your mind not to put any stumbling block or obstacle in the way of a brother or sister."*

At this point, many parents want to know how, exactly, to help them defend. Clothes can be a huge issue these days. It seems the hotter it gets, the shorter the fabric becomes, and bathing suits seem to be a tiny piece of fabric connected by dental floss these days. At one time, I did not see the big fuss in the two piece bathing suit. After all, it was "cute." Cute can cause much havoc on the eyes, the brain, and the body. Personally, I encourage parents to refrain from the two piece swim suit. How can two pieces of fabric that cover no more than a bra and panties teach our girls the point of modesty? How do we expect our boys to refrain from thinking sexual thought of our daughters when we do not ask our daughters to cover up?

The way we look can cause a physical reaction in the person looking at us and this goes both ways. Boys need to be aware of how they are showing off their well-defined chests while working out or swimming as well. The male physique can be just as distracting to a young lady as a scantily dressed girl can be to a boy. Now, the big argument is always this: *The boys are going to look regardless. Why should my daughter forego their keen sense of fashion for the sake of their fellow brothers? If the boys don't like what they are seeing, look away.* Right? Clothing or lack of clothing seems to be a touchy subject for most. Please let me remind each of you that we do not always do things because it is best for us but because it is best for another. It needs to be made clear that our day to day walk is not about us and what we want. It is what is best for the Kingdom, and sometimes that means passing up the popular clothing rack.

Along with talking to your children about why they should be modest in their dress, we also need them to understand they should be modest in their speech as well.

WALKING THE TALK

Sometimes our words, facial expressions, and the way we touch the opposite sex can be more alluring than what we are showing.

That same rule of thumb also goes for us, the parents. I cannot tell you how many times I have seen letters sent home from school instructing *parents* on how to dress when coming to school functions. We can dress "sexy" in the bedroom, but we all need to show a little modesty in our daily dress. Let's build that defensive wall strong for our brothers and sisters.

Here are a few questions you and your children can ask yourselves when getting dressed:

- What statement do my clothes make about my heart?
- Whose attention do I desire to attain? Am I seeking to please God or impress others?
- Is what I wear consistent with biblical values of modesty, self-control and respectable apparel?
- Is the Word of God my standard or is it the latest fashion?

Emotions are not always correct

The emotional roller coaster has begun - hold on tight! One day your preteen is laughing, the next day they are angry or depressed. It can be exhausting for all to endure the mood swings in this time of change. Regardless of how emotionally charged the home is at this point, we need to remember that an outburst of anger or attitude is not acceptable - for us or for them. We still need to hold our children, and ourselves, up to the standard of respect. It is also a very important time to keep the whole family grounded in God's Word.

WALKING THE TALK

It is very easy during this time of change to allow them to withdraw from the family. If we are honest, sometimes it is easier to have them holed up in their room instead of moping in the living room. Regardless of how they act, this is the time they need you. Your emotional preteen may not realize this, but it is very true – they need to stay grounded in family and not isolate.

I found this extremely difficult to do when our new homeschooling year started. It seemed wherever we lived and everywhere we made friends, my children were the opposite age and gender of everyone else's. This seemed especially true with my daughter. When our new friends did have daughters, my child was at least four years older than they were. If they were her age, they were always boys.

My daughter is now in the beginning stages of change and her emotions, at times, can be fickle. I *thought* she needed others that were going through that same season of life so she had friends she could relate to. I felt that with such a tender age coming about, she would struggle being the "only one." I was tempted to let her sit out and watch from the sidelines. But actually, I found the opposite to be true. She found freedom in her role as leader and the other little girls looked up to her. It was a great opportunity for us to teach her the importance of her character and the example she was setting. Someone was looking up to her to lead the way. That newfound responsibility empowered my daughter and challenged her to be a God-fearing example for those following her.

There are so many great lessons and opportunities for our young adults to step into if we will only keep them engaged. The last thing they need to do is to bury their heads in the sand of adolescence.

Our emotions, like our minds and bodies, are tainted because of our sin nature, and therefore emotions greatly influence us all to make selfish and foolish choices. The Bible tells us we are to be controlled by the Holy Spirit and

WALKING THE TALK

not by our emotions. If we recognize our emotions and bring them to God, we can then submit our hearts to Him and allow Him to do His work in our hearts, and let Him direct our actions. When your children have a roller coaster of emotions, don't react to them or allow them to close off. Extend grace to them, and direct them back to the Source of love, patience, and grace.

Remember to extend grace to yourself as well. We all have bad days. It is during times when we are tired, stressed, or ill that we really show our hearts to our children. Matthew 15:18 (NIV) reminds us, *"But the things that come out of a person's mouth come from the heart, and these defile them."* So guard your heart from the trap of emotions during these times and give an example to your child that will ring loud and clear in their minds when they face similar circumstances.

Questions to Ponder

If I have watched two areas where Christian parents tend to loosen the reigns, it is with dress and attitude. Be careful, parents. This is not the time to pull back and excuse their choices on adolescence.

1. Why is modesty important? Does it go beyond an attempt to prevent a physical reaction from the people looking?
2. Why should we teach our children that reacting based on our feelings is not appropriate?
3. Do you overlook or excuse your child's dress? Why must we be careful?
4. Do you brush off your children's attitude or withdrawal as a "normal "part of getting older?

Walk It Out

We all need some guidance on how we dress. Sometimes, we don't put too much thought into our choice of clothing. I know I have left the home only to find my wardrobe choice was questionable. Do a little test before leaving the house. It saves times and embarrassment (for all parties).

The Dress Test *

Question #1: *Is my shirt too short?*
Test: Raise your hands up to the sky. Does your stomach show? If so, invest in a longer shirt or ladies, wear a camisole underneath.

Question #2: *Are my jeans too low cut?*
Test: Squat down and lean over. Is it drafty? Would people mistake you for a plumber? If so, try a longer shirt or avoid low rise jeans.

Question #3: *Is my shirt too low cut?*
Test: Place your palm on your chest bone, at the base of your throat. Is there skin showing underneath your hand? If so, the shirt needs to be replaced or again, ladies, camisoles are great to add to the fabric.

Question #4: *Are my clothes too tight?*
Test: Can you comfortably sit down, squat, or bend over and breathe deeply? Would someone say it looked like you'd been poured into your clothes? Does the outline of your bra or underwear show through your shirt or pants? If so, try the next largest size, or a different style of clothes.

* If this is a group discussion, do a little fashion show. Bring some of your clothing items that you are questioning and do the test with your same-sex friends. Get honest feedback. Try this approach with your children as well.

You can also test your emotions. Emotions vary for everyone. Some of us are emotional criers or eaters. Others get angry or emotionally close down. Take a second and reflect on how you respond. How do your children handle emotions? Have you noticed any of your patterns being formed in them?

Emotions are fleeting and so is this thing we call puberty. Parents, I know that this stage of the game can be exhausting and you might be tempted to allow your children to withdraw. Let's be honest, sometimes you just want a day you don't have to battle an emotional child. I get it. Allowing our children to withdraw is extremely dangerous. More now than ever, they need to be involved with the family. When it is so easy for them to go into their shell or succumb to depression, we need to be vigilant on making sure they are engaged. Get them involved in service projects. Have them play a larger role in helping with their siblings. Get them connected in ministry at your church. *Engage* them.

You have to pick your battles, but forfeiting the fight or giving them what they want just to end tension is also extremely dangerous. Children know how far they can push you and what it will take to get you to cave. Be consistent in your discipline, and let your "yes" mean yes and your "no" mean no, no matter what their reaction may be.

WALKING THE TALK

High School

Oh, the high school years (BIG sigh). You no longer face a sweet innocent-eyed child. No, that would be too easy. You are now facing your mini-me, all too ready to prove to you they are grown up and don't need your advice. After all, they are teenagers. What else could you possibly teach them, right? The audacity of us to think that we know what they are going through!

I always get that one parent that speaks up and states that their teenager did not give them a bit of trouble. Well, congratulations. You are one in a million that successfully survived the teen years. (Please know I say this with heartfelt humor.)

Not all teenagers are difficult, but when you are addressing a young adult, you should address them with humility and respect. They have opinions and we can learn quite a lot from them if we will *listen*. All children deserve that regardless of age. I think sometimes as parents we don't see them as young adults. We still see that little boy or girl playing on the rug in a diaper eating a crayon. (You know you did, teenagers. Don't deny it. Your parents have pictures.)

When you get to this stage in the conversation, I personally believe it is not about reiterating what you have already taught them, but guiding and protecting them through real-life situations. All those conversations you had about respecting the opposite sex come into play through actions, words, and dress as they begin to date and become their own social being outside of mom and dad.

Just like we want to keep our emotionally-charged preteen connected, we should not disconnect from our teenagers. When they get to high school we think that giving them independence means totally stepping out of the picture. Please don't do that to your family. It is not necessary, parents. Your teen wants to live their own life but they also need to be able to look over their shoulder and still see you there. I know, it is a very slippery slope and one that you will not successfully navigate at all times. This is when your prayer life and time in God's word must be at its strongest.

Teens Are *Budding* Adults, Not Adults

The human brain is not fully developed until the mid-20's[3], therefore making healthy decisions difficult.
Many of us have looked at our teenagers and wondered what in the world possessed them to do what they did. We have to remember that though they look much like we do at this stage of the game, they do not necessarily think and process rewards/consequences as independently. Allowing our teens full reign because they are "adults" does not constitute a very wise decision on our parts.

"*Well, they are almost adults, I cannot always tell them what to do.*" This particular statement is like nails on a chalkboard. What makes us think we have no say in what our teens do now? I understand if they are not in your home, it can get difficult to lead them (that slippery slope emerges). Parents sometimes have joint custody of their children and discipline varies in each home. Some teens are still in high school after they turn 18 and are legally considered adults. But many things parents are allowing, legal age or not, are being done under the parent's own roofs. As long as we are their lord and master (aka shelter, food, and general provision provider) we have every right to lay down our rules and expect our teens to follow them. Making the statement "*they are adults now*" makes as much sense as saying because smoking is legal at age 18, it is okay for your 18-year-old to smoke. Is it not still dangerous?

We have a great chance to not only show our budding teenagers how to live, but *walk* with them as they begin

WALKING THE TALK

venturing out. Adulthood is scary and regardless of what they might say, your teen still needs you involved. Sometimes you will play the leader, other times the wing man. The point is that you continue to *walk* with them. It's a gradual growth and change, not a switch that is flipped just because a certain age is reached.

Boundaries Have Never Been So Important

Okay, your teen is a budding adult. Now what? Though no parent should be expected to hold their teen's hand in every situation, now more than ever is the time to enforce boundaries. Bluntly put, do not put your teens in a compromising position and then expect them to act accordingly. Again, this is a slippery slope of the teen years. Until you let them try and fail, you will never know what they are capable of, but let's use common sense.

Here's a story a woman once shared with me about the lack of enforced parental boundaries in her home. As a dating teenager, the lady's parents gave her permission to have her boyfriend in her room. The only stipulations were her parents must be home for him to be in her room and the door was to always be open. At first, the visits were innocent. The young teens talked and studied on the floor and eventually the studying moved to the bed. Less and less the parents checked in because the teens were proving to be trustworthy with their freedom. Eventually, they began making out on the bed, innocently exploring each other above the clothes. Then, one night, they had sex - door to the bedroom open, full potential to get caught if the parents decided to check on them. Let it sink in. *Two hormonally driven teenagers left in a room, alone, on a bed, without parental supervision and somehow they were supposed to make a decision that adults can hardly make with fully developed brains?* Does it make sense to anyone? I know the parents thought they were doing the right thing, but that is a slope no one needed to slide down.

When I was a teenager, I spent a lot of time with my grandparents. They traveled a lot during the summer and would allow me (and unknowingly my friends) to stay at their home. My grandparents trusted me. According to them, I was a good girl and I had not given them a reason to question my motives. It breaks my heart to think of how dishonoring I was with their trust. One time my grandparents came back early from a trip. My friends and I were in the middle of a party when they stepped into the living room. The beer cans and the glassy eyes showed them just how trustworthy I truly was as a seventeen year old.

The point is this: We all want to automatically give our teens our undivided trust, but in my opinion, it has to be earned. Even then, we, as the parents, have to remember they are teens and should not be placed in positions that could potentially be destructive. Would you leave your five year old alone without supervision? No, and we should be mindful what positions we place our teens in as well. I am not in any fashion trying to make teens out to be mindless individuals. I am, however, trying to get you to see that they still need your discernment and attention.

This goes for the electronics as well, parents. At the touch of a button, we have the world at our fingertips. So many times social media and all things electronics go unmonitored. Because we have told them to stay off certain sites or not watch that particular television show, we assume they are doing it. But do we ever go behind and check their devices or the web searches? I know some of us will read this and think *"I want them to know I trust them. Until they show me otherwise, I will believe they are doing what I taught."* Trust is earned, not an entitlement, and I encourage each of us not to turn a blind eye to the potential dangers our teens could face. By the time you realize there is a problem, your child has been looking at porn since they were thirteen or younger. The problem is much harder to address after the roots of sin have set in.

I am not encouraging you to be a helicopter parent. I am encouraging you to be hands on. I get that there is some new app or program out every single day, but we must make an effort to learn what they are viewing and from where they are obtaining their information. In my opinion, electronics have gotten out of control. Our teens have laptop computers, iPhones, tablets, etc., and somehow we are blown away by what they are doing, reading, or watching. If they are not monitored, expect something to eventually come to their attention that is harmful to them. Teens between the ages of 13-15 rank entertainment media as the top source of information about sex. [4] Did you know that teens watching television with high levels of sexual content are twice as likely to initiate sexual intercourse? Four out of five 16 year-olds regularly access pornography online and one out of three youth who viewed pornography, viewed the pornography intentionally. And maybe you do monitor and just need to put filters on the devices. After all, seven out of ten youth have accidently come across porn online. Once they see the images, they cannot be erased, accident or not. [5] Teenagers need hands-on parenting. They need to know we are still involved because we love them, so we are not going to stand idly by as they grow into the young men and women they were created to be.

CPR Listening Skills

Listening is an acquired skill. By the time your teens reach this stage, I pray that your conversations are as natural as breathing. If not, don't give up. Remember to listen. Even in their silence, your teen speaks volumes. Often times, parents will talk to fill awkward silent space because they don't know what else to do. I learned some listening skills in the counseling room that I find to be useful with teens, though they can be used with any age. Maybe you will find them useful as well. You don't have to be in the counseling room to be an active listener. Remember CPR:

Clarify: When you ask your teen a question, it gives you a chance to make sure you understand what they mean before you head down a conversational road never intended. It also gives your teen the chance to "hear" what they just said. Sometimes, when the listener says it back, the teen might see why their emotions/thoughts might not line up with truth.

Pause: Sometimes your teen might pause for a moment to collect their thoughts. That is not your cue to jump in with yours. Make sure you have something to actually say and you aren't filling up an uncomfortable silent moment with premature or unnecessary words. Dominating the conversation will easily deter your teen from sharing.

Reflect/Repeat: When your teen tells you something, let it soak in. Don't automatically respond. This will take practice. I find it helpful to repeat or paraphrase what they just said. It shows your teen you are listening and it helps *both* of you reflect on what was just said. If there are things you need to clarify before answering, this is a great time to do it.

I know you probably want concise answers for this season of life. There are not any to give. I cannot stress enough that God is your anchor as the storms rage and as you enjoy calm seas with your teen. Don't forget to talk to your Father and provide a listening ear for His directions.

Questions to Ponder

Are you anxious? As I think about the teen years looming over us, I cannot help but get butterflies. Give it to God and ask Him to show you, through His word, where you need discernment. That's what I'll be doing, for sure!

1. Have you been too complacent in your teen's life? If so, don't beat yourself up. Today is a great day to start fresh.
2. What are some other ways to protect your teen's purity during this stage of dating and freedom?
3. How can you become a better listener? Take a moment and read over these verses:

   Let every man be swift to hear, slow to speak, slow to wrath. (James 1:19)

   He who answers a matter before he hears it, it is folly and shame to him. (Prov. 18:13)

   The heart of the prudent acquires knowledge; And the ears of the wise seeks knowledge. (Prov. 18:15)

Walk It out

More now than ever before, parents need to be life affirming to one another. We are all doing our best so don't forget to encourage each other in the teen rearing years. Parenting a teen is hard work and sometimes it is trial and error. We don't always know what to do and sometimes how we handle circumstances are not the best ways. You don't have to be perfect but you need to be alert. Do not automatically ignore the small issues for one day they can become much larger.

Accountability partners are so important right now. We need to surround ourselves with friends that can speak life into our families and point out potential issues that we may not be able to see. It is hard to allow people in to help you keep check, but it takes a village, right? Make sure you continue talking to your spouse and ensure you are both on the same page as far as discipline, boundaries, and freedoms. Now more than ever, ensuring you are both in agreement on how to raise your teen is vital. This is a time that you should stick together. You have made it this far so don't give up now!

Chapter Five: Mixed Messages

There is a saying, *"Don't do what I do. Do what I say."* Sadly, it is an approach I believe is literally destroying our families. Our lifestyles often do not line up with the lip service that is flowing from our mouths. No wonder our children are so confused. The conundrums we use with our children are endless. Remember I told you that clarity is very important? Here are a few examples of what I mean by mixed messages:

Example #1: Our daughters want to wear makeup. When they ask if they can, we exclaim, *"Oh darling, you don't need that makeup on your face. You are beautiful."* I don't know about you, but I have *so* used that line on my daughter. But before makeup lovers boycott me, let me say I don't have anything against makeup. I have strong opinions on when makeup on young girls is appropriate, but I will refrain from sharing – it's really a personal choice.

Here's the mixed part of the message: *They don't need makeup because they are beautiful, then why do you wear it? Are you not just as beautiful?* My guess is you have never thought about it. Some of you are thinking, *"Great, Sarah, one more thing for me to consider."* I use this example to show how we, as parents, need to be mindful on how we approach topics. We cannot be truthful and contradictory in the same sentence. A better way to approach that question might be like this: *"The rule in our home is makeup cannot be worn until [age]. I appreciate you asking me before wearing it."*

Example #2: A father and son are attending a football game. The cheerleader's uniforms leave very little to the imagination. They are cheering directly in front of where the father and son are sitting. The father begins making inappropriate comments to his son about the cheerleader's curves. The comments are innocent in nature and they get a little laugh out of the jokes. Great father and son bonding moment, right? Maybe not – ask his wife how she feels about it.

We tell our children to respect the opposite sex, to honor their spouses, and to protect their eyes from things of the flesh. Then we go and do something like what I just described without thinking of the mixed message we're sending. The father's comments were not respectful of the opposite sex, they were not honoring to his wife, and he definitely did not help his son protect his eyes nor his heart...all with the intent of some father/son bonding.

Example #3: I really want you to understand this mixed message we often send about purity. We tell our sons and daughters not to have sex until they are married. Then, as they get older and begin dating, we get fearful they might succumb to the urges and have sex. For safety measures, we tell them not to have sex...but if for some reason they do, make sure they use protection. I will go a step further and say we also tell them they should at least love the other person and be engaged. I cannot tell you how many parents I have heard excuse their child's sexual immorality because their son or daughter was "engaged" to the person with whom they were sexually active. Engagement is not a green flag to go ahead and *act* married. It is a time to get to know one another and ensure that marriage is the best next step.

Okay parents, listen up – here's the bottom line. The mixed message of purity is this: *Don't do it, but if you do, be safe.* This message is like telling a drug addict: *Don't use drugs, but if you do, use a clean needle.*

I could go on and on about the mixed messages we unintentionally send our children. We say that God is in control, yet we worry and fret over every aspect of our lives. We say God is love, but we treat our spouses with hostility

WALKING THE TALK

and have hatred in our hearts for our brother. We surrender on Sundays and live like the world the rest of the week. If you are doing this, are you really that surprised that your children don't know what to do? Is it much of a surprise that they give God only the parts they want Him to have and keep the rest?

Here's what Jesus had to say about mixed messages. *"These people draw near to Me with their mouth, and honor Me with their lips, but their heart is far from Me. And in vain they worship Me, Teaching as doctrines the commandments of men." (Matthew 15:8)*

We all need to be much more intentional about our lives, and that our actions and words don't contradict each other. The next two sections contain ways teens can be damaged or confused by their parents' mixed messages. Before you start the next section, meditate on the previous examples of mixed messages. Are you guilty of sending any of these messages to your child?

Purity:
1. Recognize that sex is good; don't make it bad.
2. Understand that virginity is not an indicator of a pure heart.

Prodigals:
1. Learn how to deal with a wayward child, and that sometimes, our parental guidance won't be heeded.

Purity: A Few Misunderstandings

In our attempt to keep our children pure, many parents have only focused on one side of the purity message: the DON'T message. DON'T have sex because you will get pregnant. DON'T have sex because you will get a disease. DON'T have sex because God said so. Trust me, I believe the ramifications of sex outside God's design are important to discuss, but there's another key part of the message we are failing to share: God does not just want our sexual purity, He wants purity in *all things*.

Pure thoughts. Pure words. Pure actions. Pure choices.

Parents, I get it. We want our children to wait, and sometimes we will use about any tactic to convince them it's the right thing to do. A word of caution: we need to be careful treading this ground. Children and especially young adults can have extremely distorted views on why they are waiting until their wedding night. If they do wait, many of them are highly disappointed. Why? *Reality* and *fantasy* are very different. I want to make this clear. Christians have been called to uphold a particular lifestyle. But somewhere in our "true love waits" talks and "purity commitment" cards we have missed the point of *why* they should wait.

We want our children to conform to God's way because of their love and obedience for God. Though that obedience requires a response, in this case celibacy, our actions alone, no matter how great they might be, cannot replace the true intent of our hearts. In other words, the *why* behind our actions is more important than just refraining from sex.

Here are some misunderstandings I've heard about purity and the reasons for waiting. I hope that by reading these you will remember that though these may be good points, they cannot replace *the* point about living an overall life of purity.

Misunderstanding #1: Our long suffering and self-denial will be rewarded by a passionate marriage.

Teens and young adults have been inundated with this idea that if you remain a virgin until your wedding night, God will bless your marriage with *mind-blowing* sex and a blissful marriage. Great idea, but it is very misleading (and not the goal of marriage...which is a whole other topic). The message of sexual purity is being presented like a trade-off. We (parents, educators, ministers) are unknowingly conveying to our children that if they will abstain from sexual immorality, God, in return, will provide them an adoring spouse and a passionate, disease-free sex life.

He's God, not a genie. And our lives are not about us, but about *Him*.

Some of you might be scratching your head. Shouldn't we tell our children that God wants them to have a good marriage? Shouldn't we tell our children that a lot of heartache can be avoided in our relationships by doing it the way God designed? Yes, but no. Again, we put too much emphasis on the personal, physical gratification and ramifications of sex.

Scripture tells us that we are not to be unequally yoked. In hard times, when even sex won't fix the issues, two Christians that are focused on obeying God in their personal and spiritual lives will weather a storm much easier than two unequally yoked persons. In order for our teens to enjoy the bliss of marriage, they first need to be in a union that is focused on God. Sex is just an added benefit.

But what about people who don't get married? Is that command from God to flee from sexual immorality null and void because they decide not to pursue life with a partner? Are they free to do as they please? Scripture tells us that our bodies do not belong to us. Our bodies are temples, bought at a price by God (1 Corinthians 6:18-20). The price was the blood of God's only Son, Jesus. Yes, God designed sex for the marriage bed, but the concept of our bodies belonging to God is much deeper. Refraining from the carnal desires of our flesh outside of God's design signifies our *obedience* to *Him*, regardless if we ever get married or not. We need to teach our children that we abstain from sex outside of marriage, not because of what we may or may not get in return, but because we are called to be obedient to the One that our bodies belong to.

Misunderstanding #2: Successfully holding on to their virginity will make them a better Christian.

I read an article one time titled "It Happened to Me: I Saved My Virginity for My Wedding and I Regretted It."[6] I want to share an excerpt from her article that will hopefully make my pointer crystal clear on this particular misunderstanding. The author wrote:

"I stood in the hotel bathroom beforehand, wearing my white lingerie, thinking, "I made it. I'm a good Christian." There was no chorus of angels, no shining light from Heaven. It was just me and my husband in a dark room, fumbling with a condom and a bottle of lube for the first time."

I know a lot of people, men and women, who were virgins when they got married, and it had nothing to do with their faith. I know a lot of Christians who didn't wait. Do we really want our children to gauge their Christian walk on just their virginity? We should be teaching our children that when they are focused on God's instruction, their actions will follow. When we are seeking spiritual purity out of our obedience to Christ, the physical, emotional and mental purity will fall into its place.

I understand that it's easy to measure our religious progress by what we are doing or not doing. But people mess up, and I'm afraid it's because of this "measure" mentality that those who did miss the mark are so afraid to come back to the herd. Let's introduce our children to the concept of grace: we are Christians because of what Jesus did, not because of what *we* do (or don't do). Grace becomes real to our kids as we live it out before them. It is during these times, as we struggle, they learn the importance of leaning on a strength that only comes from our Heavenly Father.

Misunderstanding #3: Good Girls Don't

"Good girls don't" is all that my friend's mother told her about sex. The statement, as you can imagine, left her confused as a young girl. Good girls don't what?

> *Good girls don't have longing and desire?*
> *Good girls don't struggle with sexual purity?*
> *Good girls don't want to have sex?*

What don't good girls do?

I am sure many of you have heard the analogy of the fireplace. Fire, when kept in its proper place, can provide warmth and illumination. Fire outside of its proper place can lead to destruction and harm. Parents, let's not forget to talk about how sex can be a wonderful thing in its proper place: marriage. Sex is not a bad thing, it's a normal thing. Sex isn't something only perverted, bad people want to do. Sex is beautiful and should be celebrated, not shamed. God created sex to be enjoyed by a man and woman within the confines of marriage.

I heard the "don't" purity message often. Imagine how I struggled (along with all the other teens) when I still *wanted* to have sex. Was there something wrong with me? Was I a bad person because I still had those longings and desires? Now, after years of struggling with intimacy, I understand I was a normal teenage girl coming into her own. But my internal message of purity was so distorted I kept all my questions and struggles to myself. When I became sexually active, I hid it; and I constantly struggled with the shame. I couldn't talk with anyone because I felt I should not have these sexual urges in the first place. I knew if other teens found out about me, it would hurt my influence. I was stuck between doing what I desired and doing what was expected.

The longer I held in my shame, the farther I walked away from God and His instruction. In church, I always felt like a hypocrite. In my eyes, there was nothing I could give to God. I was already tarnished. Why even try to be anything else? Oh, how I wish I could go back and tell myself that regardless of how far I had gone, I could always come back to my Father. My shame kept me shackled and silent in my struggles. And my shame followed me into my marriage.

My sexual ventures were done in secret for so long because of the shame attributed to sex outside of marriage that when I could *rightfully* share in sexual union with my husband, I still struggled with feelings of it being "wrong." A girlfriend of mine explained it the best to me: as teens, we are told NO for so long about sex that we feel wrong saying YES in our marriage bed. As a wife and mother, I felt like I could not be sexual. When I felt the longings for my husband and tried to express myself sexually, I felt dirty. I couldn't shake the feeling that God was disgusted with me. So, for a long time, I avoided sex with my husband.

I carried a lot of shame into my marriage because of my poor decisions and I will be the first one to admit that I had a distorted view of what marriage was to be like. Expectations were put on my husband that no man, no matter how great he is, could ever come to satisfy. My past brought shame and I tried very hard to rectify my past by making my marriage honorable. The key factor, however,

WALKING THE TALK

was not there and it showed. My husband and I were married nine years before I was saved, and we had a marriage foundation that could stand up to the pressures. It was when I was saved that I understood grace and I realized that my past no longer held any part of me prisoner. For the first time, I saw a God that was not out to shame me, but to love me. When I realized that I was beautiful in my Father's eyes, I learned to love myself. God slowly changed me from the inside out and as I grew in my walk with God, my marriage grew. Eventually I learned to eagerly participate in the sex life that I had once so dreaded!

God designed us to have sexual longings. It is the way a married couple bonds. It is also is another reason that sex should not be discussed as something that is only physical. Here goes that triune idea again. The bond that is shared between husband and wife during sex is spiritual, emotional, and mental as well as physical. It connects you to someone else on the most intimate of levels. We can't be "connecting" sexually with others outside marriage and not experience the hurtful severing of such an intimate bond. The relational bond God uniquely created to be experienced during sex should be celebrated and not shamed.

Misunderstanding #4: Purity Is Only for Girls

I will admit something to each of you reading this part - I can be somewhat biased in the discussion of purity. Honestly, I do not mean to be, but since the physical ramifications are so much more extreme on young ladies I tend to focus on them more than the men. Regardless if we mean to or not, I think we all know this fact surrounding women to be true; therefore, much of our time and words are spent on keeping our young ladies pure. We tell them that God has a husband for them and it is their duty to

WALKING THE TALK

remain chaste for him and their wedding night (misunderstanding #1).

Unfortunately, we forget there is a young man somewhere in that picture that should be encouraged to walk a path of purity as well. Too often, while we are telling a girl to wait, young men are getting the opposite message. We laugh and joke about how the girls swoon over them. Women and alcohol are almost an unspoken rite of passage for him because he is *"just being a guy."* Society (and parents) condones the same behaviors from a man that would be highly condemned for a woman. Maybe it is not on purpose, but it is happening. The message of purity is for both genders and it is equally important. And again, the message of purity has never been just about sex - that is a misunderstanding.

As parents, our job is to help our children understand the beauty of what they have to give to their future spouse and the importance of protecting and saving it for marriage. As I have already stated, when a person knows that something has value, they are more likely to protect it from harm or loss. Until we, as parents, can see it like this, I am afraid the mixed purity message will leave our children confused, torn and left without all the information they need to make an informed choice.

God wants men and women alike to have pure hearts, not just be pure from the outside. In order to have a pure heart, our hearts must seek God and only God. We want our men and women to be seekers of purity in all areas of their lives. *Pure thoughts. Pure words. Pure actions. Pure choices.*

WALKING THE TALK

Questions to Ponder

Hanging in there? You are doing great! The mixed messages about purity hopefully made you stop and think about what we are telling our children. I hope you also see the importance of understanding how God desires a relationship built from our love and obedience.

1. What is obedience?
2. How does obedience affect your day-to-day activities and thoughts?
3. Reflect on how your understanding of obedience could affect the talk with your child (boundaries, inappropriate touching, oral sex).
4. Are we telling our boys and girls two different messages?

Walk It Out

Obedience is an attitude of heart toward a higher authority. As Christians, that higher authority is God Himself. The Lord said in John 14:15, *"If you love Me, keep My commandments."* It also deals with the individual's own attitude toward God. Many people follow a law in fear of punishment; however their attitude is certainly not one of obedience. Many young adults might choose to wait to have sex until marriage out of fear of pregnancy, disease, or disappointing parents; but their hearts are not doing it out of obedience. They might follow a rule/law to avoid punishment; however the peace and joy that comes from obedience is not there. Trust me, it makes the decision to abstain much harder.

This is where gray areas usually happen. Professing believers may not engage in full sexual activity, but they tend to push the boundaries. How far is too far? I have found throughout my time in youth groups and the counseling room that many young believers have a major disconnect when it comes to sexual intercourse and oral sex. They might hold to their virginity, but compromise on every other area (oral sex, inappropriate touching, masturbation, porn). We, as parents, must make clear that God calls us to purity in *all* areas. Furthermore, you must know where you stand on these topics before you can address them. You can do it! Hang in there!

Here are a few passages that I think really help us wrap our minds around what purity is and how we seek it in our day to day lives. Take a moment and read over them. See how you can use them in your home with your sons and daughters.

Psalm 119:9:   *"How can a young man cleanse his way? By taking heed according to Your word."*

WALKING THE TALK

Matthew 5:8: *"Blessed are the pure in heart, for they shall see God."*

Psalm 51:10: *"Create in me a clean heart, O god. And renew a steadfast spirit within me."*

Titus 2:12: *"Teaching us that, denying ungodliness ad worldly lusts, we should live soberly, righteously and godly in the present age."*

The Wayward Child

No one tells you just how difficult parenting can be. At times, being a mother has made me feel extremely isolated and defeated. Do others feel like their good enough just isn't, well, good enough? If I am honest, I often find myself analyzing my children, picking out personality traits that could be potential issues when they get older. For example, my daughter loves the spotlight and my son tends to withdraw emotionally when he is dealing with an issue. My mind will start questioning if I have properly prepared them for the world at hand. When I am no longer around, will they stand firm or fall short? Will my daughter's love of the spotlight cause her to compromise herself to get that attention? Will my son fall in with the wrong crowd because he tends to follow instead of lead? It is easy to look at those concerns I just voiced and think I am extreme, but how many parents worry about that very thing?

We worry about the future fate of our children that has not happened yet sometimes neglect the days we have been given to speak life into our children.

I was sharing with a friend during a lunch date that all I hope for my children is they choose an easier path than I did. I will pass along the advice that dear friend shared with me. With much love and truth, she told me that I had no control over what my children would do when they got older. All I could do was point them to Christ and pray that a solid foundation had been laid for them. She went on to remind me that we had to give our children's past, present, and future to God and trust that even if they did mess up, He could still use that stumble for His purpose. She then gingerly took my hand and reminded me He was using me.

I know many of you are on the verge of the teen years with your children. Some of you have already started the rocky journey. And maybe even for a few, you have survived "teen-hood" with very little casualty. Regardless of where you are, I want the words I am going to share to stand as a reminder that your role, however difficult and sometimes faltering, is valuable.

And for the parents who are struggling with a wayward child, as many of you may be, what I am about to write might be hard for you to read and even harder to accept. From working with teenagers, and from being a prodigal teen myself, I can, with much certainty, tell you that you need to let yourselves off the hook and stop taking the entire blame for your teenager's rebellion.

I wrote a letter I will share from the perspective of a wayward teen. I am sure many of you have been reading this guide and thinking, *"I did everything right. We taught the importance of healthy relationships, God was first priority and yet here we are, with a son/daughter that continues to defy his/her upbringing."* I get emails from parents in this same scenario, and I understand. Life doesn't always make sense and the outcome we had hoped for doesn't always come to fruition. Sometimes, marriages are broken and you are left trying to raise a godly son or daughter alone. You are struggling and don't quite know if there is another way. Please listen when I say that God is in the business of working life miracles. If we will hand over our lives to Him, and trust Him with the lives of our children, He can be honored in our family. God can be honored through a bad marriage, through illness, through financial difficulty, through rebellion and through our weaknesses. Don't ever forget that.

Here's a letter for parents from a wandering child.

Dear Mom and Dad,
I need you to remember three things:
I made a choice, not you.
I'm sure you wonder how that could be. Every day, you were at home when I got off the school bus with a smile and

a healthy snack. You read books to me at night and said my bedtime prayers with me. At every school sporting event, you were there, proudly chasing me around with the camcorder. Our home provided security and created happy memories. Yet, when you weren't around, I made choices that hurt you and me. Please understand it has nothing to do with you and is no reflection of your success or failure as my parent. *I am sure this is difficult to accept, but regardless of how great a parent you have been to me, I still must make decisions for myself. Sometimes, I choose the wrong thing. It's part of growing up.*

Your faith can't be my faith.

Every Sunday, you held my hand and lead me to Sunday school. At every meal, we prayed, thanking God for the bounty in front of us. John 3:16 was a staple Scripture in our home. I was so young and still learning. But you were strong in your faith and your love for God shined brightly. Yet, as I grew older, I started to waver in my walk. You tried so hard to bring me back into the fold. You rarely left your knees during those rebellious times for me; still, I went into the world. I know you want me to come back to God, but I must first know who God is to me. My relationship with God must be personal. Your faith won't save me. *Please keep praying for me. That is all you can do.*

Sometimes to love me, you must let me fall.

I know you want to fix everything in life that goes wrong for me. You don't want to see me suffer any more than I have to. There is a fine line between enabling and loving. When you constantly "save" me from myself, you aren't really helping me grow up. I'm sure that when I get in trouble, it's embarrassing to you and all you want to do is sweep it under the rug, to forget the transgression and move on. But when you do, I don't learn my lesson; I learn how to make excuses. *Please tell me "no" and let me figure out life on my own. I might say hurtful things like "you just don't care about me" or "if you really loved me" but trust me when I say I am*

WALKING THE TALK

immature and trying to avoid the consequences that my choices brought upon me. Until you allow me to fall and reap the consequences, I will always see myself as the victim.

Mom and Dad, please stop obsessing about what you could have done differently. There are many roads you could have taken in your parenting journey, none of them promise a different result.

Please keep loving me and continue praying for me to return.

Until then,
The Wayward Child

Thoughts to Ponder

Many of you are now facing a rebellious teen. Some of you will relate to this section because you were, at one time, the prodigal. If you are reading this now, I hope God is working in your life and I pray He will continue to strengthen and encourage you in this season of your walk.

1.   Can you relate to the story of the wayward child? What side of the story were you?
2.   If you are a parent dealing with a wayward child, do you deal with doubt or guilt?
3.   What scripture verses can bring you comfort in this season with your child?
4.   Take a look at Luke 15:11- 32. We know the prodigal son leaves his father, squanders all his money, only to return home. How did the father respond to his wayward son? What can we learn from them?

Walk It Out

When I shared the idea for this book with some people and explained the premise that it is our relationships and examples that our children must see, a common response was, "Oh, that is great, but I had godly parents and I still turned out bad." If you are dealing with a child that veered far off the path you so desperately tried to get him/her to walk, please take comfort in the fact God can still use that child for His glory. I would not be writing this book had I, myself, not gone down some not-so-good streets. The point of the letter is to remind you that God is in control. We do not have the power to convict or to save our children. I know that is hard for many of us, but I hope you find comfort in knowing that God did not intend for us to do life alone. He has placed you, hopefully, in a life affirming group of believers that will love and encourage you. If you do not have that, let me encourage you to seek it out in a church home.

If you are struggling with guilt or fear about your child, take a moment and meditate on these scripture verses. May God bring you peace in the storm you are facing. These five verses will get you started:

You are safe with God.
God is our refuge and strength, A very present help in trouble. – Psalm 46:1

God is in control.
He calms the storm, so the waves are still. – Psalm 107:29

God will rescue you.
The righteous call out and the Lord hears, and delivers them out of all their troubles. – Psalm 34:17

WALKING THE TALK

You can always trust in God as your protector.
He who dwells in the secret place of the Most High shall abide under the shadow of the Most High. I will say of the Lord, "He is my refuge and my fortress- My God, in Him I will trust. – Psalm 91:1-2

God will give you strength.
And He said to me, "My grace is sufficient for you, for My strength is made perfect in your weakness."
– 2 Corinthians 12:9

Chapter Six: A Call to Pray

Do you have a burden you are trying to carry that you need to give to your Heavenly Father?

My prayer for you at this point is that you have gleaned insight from the book and from one another (if you've had a chance to discuss the questions). I do pray that you see the value of your role, regardless of what others might tell you or how you might sometimes feel.

You are needed.

You are called.

Whether you are in a small group or reading this book alone, I encourage you to take this time to pray for your children. Pray for your marriage (or your singleness). Pray for discernment in your season of life. Pray for a continually renewed relationship with your Heavenly Father.

Don't forget that we need time with God *every* day. If we are going to face all that life throws at us, we need to be grounded in our faith, our focus must be on God, and our hearts must be attuned to His will.

Prayer time is such an important part of our lives and sometimes I think it is downplayed. It often takes the backseat to our everyday schedules, hurdles, and distractions. But our time with God should be how we start and end our days. *Prayer is life changing.*

I can attest to prayer's power. It has been during my quiet moments that God's Spirit spoke and I heard it. During my hours of prayer, God finally silenced all the noise in my heart and replaced that noise with a calm that can only be attributed to being His child. And it was while I was on my hands and knees practicing religion (performing) during my early years of marriage that I found a relationship with God.

We need a certain time to come before God and let everything else wait. Find a moment in the day that you can spend five, ten, fifteen minutes of quiet time with God. I highly recommend mornings before your days get hectic with school and work. Pray over the day's schedule. Pray over your children, their schools, their teachers and their friends. Take a moment and ask God to show you what He wants you to do during that day.

God, give me eyes to see and ears to hear.

A consistent place to go and pray is also helpful. Jesus had a prayer place. Mark 1:35 reads, *"Very early in the morning, while it was still dark, Jesus got up, left the house and went off to a solitary place where He prayed."* I usually get my coffee, turn on some worship music, go outside on the porch and talk to my Father. I don't always have much to say and sometimes the only words I utter are, *"Lord, I trust you. I give this day to You."* After all, God is not looking for your solutions. He simply wants to know that You are looking to Him.

Lord, I look to You, sustainer of life and my provision.

I provided a few prayers on the following pages to help you get started. Pray as you feel led. These prayers are just suggestions. Your needs might be very different from mine or from the person seated next to you. God knows your heart. He knows your needs, your desires and your longings. Give your requests to Him and trust His will to be done in your life and in your children's lives.

WALKING THE TALK

Prayer for Marriage

Dear Lord,

We commit our marriage to You. We pray, Father, that our union can serve as a testimony of the covenant we each share with You.

Help me to show grace to my spouse, even when it is not deserved. Remind each of us of your mercy and love so that we can bestow that same mercy and love to one another.

Father, forgive us for our self-centeredness, anger, lust, and foolish quarrels. Help us keep our eyes trained on You, the source of all things pure and lovely.

If there are areas in our marriage that need healing, we ask that You mend our hearts. We ask that you take the blinders of pride and selfishness off our eyes so we see Your truth and stop following our own opinions.

We pray for Your protection over our marriage. Keep and deliver us from the enemy that wants nothing more than to destroy our marriage.

Lord, surround us with godly counsel. Draw us into Your Word so that we can receive your wisdom and will for our lives.

We entrust you, Lord, with our marriage.

Amen.

Prayer for Single Parents

Dear Lord,

I come before you humbled. My life has not turned out the way I imagined, but I am thankful for your ever present hand upon it. Thank you, Lord, for your provision, peace, and protection.

Remind me in my days of doubt, and in my times of unfair comparison, unforgiveness, and anger that You are a Father of love and mercy. Soften my heart toward my children's (father/mother). Help me extend to them the same love and forgiveness you have bestowed upon me.

Lord, help me not to respond to my ex in spite or strife. If one of us is lacking in Your knowledge, please convict our hearts and draw us near to You. Lord, I pray that both of us desire to be godly parents, leading our children in truth. Regardless Lord, I ask for Your hand to be upon our children. Help me bring them up in Your Word so that even when they are old they will not depart from it.

Father, I believe that you can take a storm and make a rainbow. Thank you for your provision.

I offer my body as a living and holy sacrifice that is pure in every aspect. I am Your bride and You are my first love.

Thank you for your unconditional love and grace toward my family.

Amen.

Prayer for Children

Dear Lord,

I thank you for entrusting me with such beauty and innocence. Father, it can be so scary to think of the things that could go wrong raising children in this world. I pray Lord that you will replace my fear and doubt with boldness and confidence. I ask that Your hand be upon my children.

Lord, I pray that they come to know You in an intimate relationship and that they grow in Your grace. I pray they seek Your will and not their own. Father, help my children not to be like those around them, but use them as salt and light in a world that has lost its flavor and direction. Give them boldness, Lord, to speak your truth, even when it is not popular.

Surround them with godly counsel and seekers of Your truth. Create in them a pure heart that overflows with kindness and generosity so that others around them see You through their actions. I pray that their faith will grow and they will be used as a Kingdom catalyst in their friendships, their schools, their churches, and their communities. Set them apart, Lord, for Your divine calling on their life.

I thank you for the honor You have given me as their father/mother. I ask humbly, Lord, that Your hand guide and protect us. Even when things get hard or the path is unclear, please remind us of Your promise that You will never leave us nor forsake us.

Thank you for being my Father.
Amen.

Thoughts to Ponder

1.   How often do you pray for your marriage? Your children?
2.   Do you have a consistent prayer life? What changes might God have you make?

Walk It Out

Write a prayer to God about what you'd like Him to help you with as a response to reading this book.

Appendix A

Test Your Knowledge Quiz

We cannot avoid pertinent information pertaining to teen pregnancy and STIs (sexually transmitted infections). After all, knowledge is power. As a group or by yourself, test your knowledge. Consider it a crash course on pregnancy and STIs, just without the grade!

1. There are _____ number of STIs.
    a. 15   b. 25   c. 32   d. other

2. What is the leading STI for sexually active teens?
    a. AIDS   b. gonorrhea c. genital warts

3. True or False: There are two types of STIs.

4. How can a person contract a STI?

5. True or False: When a person contracts a venereal disease, they always have symptoms.

6. Average age of a teen pregnancy.
    a. 15   B. 12   C. 20

7. True or False: Condoms prevent the transmission of all STIs.

8. What is the failure rate of birth control pills?
    a. 3-5% b. 1-2%   c. 14-15%

9. What is the failure rate of condoms?
    a. 3-5% b. 1-2%   c. 14-15%

10. Is the withdrawal or "pull out" method a safe method to use to prevent pregnancy? Why?

Answer Key [7]

1. In the 1950's, there were two know STIs - Syphilis and Gonorrhea. Today, there are anywhere from 25-30 different sexually transmitted infections.

2. Human papillomavirus (HPV) is the most common sexually transmitted infection in the United States. [8] Chlamydia is a common sexually transmitted disease (STD) that can be easily cured. If left untreated, chlamydia can make it difficult for a woman to get pregnant.[9]

3. True: There are two categories that STIs fall in - Bacterial and Viral. Bacterial STIs are treatable if discovered in time. Viral STIs can be treated for symptoms but is not curable.

4. Both viral and bacterial STIs can be transmitted from a partner by anal, oral, or vaginal contact. Bodily secretions can transmit a bacterial infection. Viral STIs are transmitted by skin to skin contact with a partner.

5. An infected person does not always have symptoms. In fact, 75 percent of women infected with chlamydia never have symptoms. When a person is asymptomatic, there is the risk of higher transmission rate between partners (if they have/had multiple partners). Chlamydia and gonorrhea when left untreated can cause Pelvic Inflammatory Disease (PID).

6. Teen Pregnancy in the United States: In 2013, a total of 273,105 babies were born to women aged **15–19 years**, for a live birth rate of 26.5 per 1,000 women in this age group.[10] In 2010, teen pregnancy and childbirth accounted for at least $9.4 billion in costs to U.S. taxpayers for increased health care and

foster care, increased incarceration rates among children of teen parents, and lost tax revenue because of lower educational attainment and income among teen mothers.

Pregnancy and birth are significant contributors to high school dropout rates among girls. Only about 50 percent of teen mothers receive a high school diploma by 22 years of age, versus approximately 90 percent of women who had not given birth during adolescence.

The children of teenage mothers are more likely to have lower school achievement and drop out of high school, have more health problems, be incarcerated at some time during adolescence, give birth as a teenager, and face unemployment as a young adult.

7. False: When condoms are used properly they can provide some but not complete protection.

8. Birth control has a failure rate of 3-5 percent. The reasons for its failure include (but are not limited to) failure to take consistently. Antibiotics can cancel out birth control.

9. Condoms have a failure rate of 14-15 percent. Condoms do not protect from viral STIs because they are transmitted by skin to skin contact. Condoms do not cover the entire genital area. Condoms also fail because they are not the proper size and their storage renders it from effectively protecting as it was intended. Condoms also expire.

10. Before a man ejaculates, there is a pre-emission fluid that is released. The fluid is clear but contains sperm.

WALKING THE TALK

Endnotes

Chapter One

1. Kevin DeYoung. "Premarital Sex and Our Love Affair with Bad Stats." http://www.thegospelcoalition.org/blogs/kevin deyoung/2011/12/13/premarital-sex-and-our-love-affair-with-bad-stats/ (August 2015)

Chapter Two

2. "Facts and TV Stats: 'It's Just Harmless Entertainment.' Oh Really?" http://www.parentstv.org/PTC/facts/mediafac ts.asp (September 2015)

Chapter Four

3. Joe S. McIlhaney, Freda McKissic Bush. *Hooked: New Science on How Casual Sex is Affecting Our Children.* (Northfield Publishing: 2008).

4. Anne Klockenkemper. "Sexual Media, Sexual Teens." http://iml.jou.ufl.edu/projects/Spring02/Kloc kenkemper/page2.htm (August, 2015).

5. "Enough Is Enough. Internet Safety 101." http://www.internetsafety101.org/pornograph ystatistics.htm. (August, 2015).

Chapter Five

6. Samantha Pugsley. "It Happened to Me: I Waited to Lose My Virginity On My Wedding Night and Wish I Hadn't." http://www.xojane.com/sex/true-love-waits-pledge (August, 2014).

Appendix A

7. Center for Disease Control and Prevention. Sexually Transmitted Diseases (STDs). http://www.cdc.gov/std/default.htm. (September 2015).

8. Center for Disease Control and Prevention. Genital HPV Infection - Fact Sheet. http://www.cdc.gov/std/hpv/stdfact-hpv.htm. (September 2015).

9. Center for Disease Control and Prevention. CDC Fact Sheet http://www.cdc.gov/std/hpv/stdfact-hpv.htm. (August 2015).

10. Center for Disease Control and Prevention. About Teen Pregnancy. http://www.cdc.gov/teenpregnancy/about/index.htm. (August 2015).

WALKING THE TALK

WALKING THE TALK

WALKING THE TALK